The Ansbacher Conspiracy

The Ansbacher Conspiracy

Colm Keena

Gill & Macmillan

Gill & Macmillan Ltd
Hume Avenue, Park West, Dublin 12
with associated companies throughout the world
www.gillmacmillan.ie
© Colm Keena 2003
0 7171 3564 0
Design and print origination by Carole Lynch
Printed by ColourBooks Ltd, Dublin

This book is typeset in Goudy 10.5 on 14.5 pt.

*The paper used in this book comes from the wood pulp of
managed forests. For every tree felled, at least one tree
is planted, thereby renewing natural resources.*

A CIP catalogue record for this book is available
from the British Library.

1 3 5 4 2

All photographs included in this book are supplied
by courtesy of *The Irish Times*, except that of Patrick Gallagher
which is by courtesy of the Charlie Collins Agency.

for
Feargha, Conor and Ruairí

'It was politic to give some work to Haughey Boland.'
Businessman and Fianna Fáil fundraiser, Ken O'Reilly-Hyland,
speaking about the 1960s in an interview with the
Ansbacher inspectors on 22 June 2000.

'Then I got a kind of an indication that the State was interested in it for a
court... That is the only reason I took a chance on the development.'
Businessman, solicitor and Fianna Fáil fundraiser, Gerald Hickey,
referring to his purchase of Dolphin House, East Essex Street,
Temple Bar, Dublin, in an interview with the
Ansbacher inspectors on 25 May 2000.

Contents

PART FIVE Things Fall Apart

Introduction

Number 17 College Green, Dublin, was built in 1931 by Guinness & Mahon bank to house the operations of what was already one of the oldest banks in Ireland. On the ground floor is a banking hall with a high ceiling and modestly ornate plasterwork. At the back of the hall a doorway leads to a corridor, back offices and a winding narrow stairway which leads down to the basement. The basement rooms have thick walls and some have heavy steel-barred doors, such as you might see attached to the cells at the back of a sheriff's office in an old cowboy movie. One room has a thick steel door and a steel-barred door. In the old days you had to open both before you could get into the thick-walled basement room where two heavy steel safes stood on high brick pedestals designed to protect them from flooding. Other steel-doored rooms also held safes. Whoever was in charge of these rooms had an impressive collection of keys.

The basement of the building stretches out under the pavement and road in College Green. These days you can hear the rumble of the traffic overhead when you are poking around the mostly abandoned rooms. Some of the rooms have no bulbs in the light fixtures and you have to use a torch. In the corner of the largest room there is what used to be a kitchen. There's a sink, a Formica-covered worktop and an old white microwave. In another room there's a loading bay and what used to be the door to a dumb waiter or small lift that went up through the building. The loading bay was built so that it could accommodate heavy loads, a safe perhaps, or large containers of documents. No-one who works in the building now knows.

At the back of the basement there is a large, thick-walled room where the Guinness & Mahon (G&M) archives were stored. Banks, of course, need to keep good records in case a mistake is made and a customer later questions what has happened to his or her money. Banks can follow money as it makes its way through the banking system. In G&M each payment or amount of money that came into the bank was given a transaction code. When an amount of money was transferred from one account to another within the bank, that transaction was also given a code. When money left the bank a note would appear in the accounts showing where the money went, and whether it was given out in cash, cheque, or by electronic transfer. When cheques are cashed they are returned to the issuing bank for clearance, and banks keep copies of the cheques, which are usually also stamped by the receiving bank. In this way a record is kept of where the cheque goes, and the money trail can be picked up in the receiving bank, which would have allocated a transaction code to the lodgement of the cheque.

As well as helping customers with queries about their accounts, these procedures can help investigators who are trying to follow a money trail to see who received or issued a particular amount of money. The money trail has often scuppered the attempts of wrong-doers to hide or deny their wrongdoing. Bank records can be powerful weapons in the hands of inquisitors.

Many of the larger banks, because of the enormous amounts of documentation they accumulate, operate a limited retention policy. In other words, they destroy many documents after a set period of years. G&M, because it was a relatively small bank, did not destroy records. It kept everything. From the early 1970s, all G&M transactions were entered into the bank's computer system. Printouts of transactions across accounts were stored in large ring-bound folders and every few months the records were sent off to be transferred onto microfiche, before being stored in the basement archives. These old archives, which for years gathered dust in the basement of Number 17 College Green, held some of the most sensitive political secrets of their day.

In recent years the public's view of what happened in the Irish Republic during the 1970s, 1980s and 1990s has been changed by a series of financial revelations. Most people at the time viewed the quarter century up to the mid-1990s as a financially difficult period. In the early 1970s the economy was hit hard by questionable economic policies and the global effects of the oil crisis. The years that followed saw crippling levels of taxation, with workers on quite moderate incomes paying huge proportions of their earnings in tax. They got little in return in terms of public services.

The dominant political figure of this period was the former Taoiseach and leader of Fianna Fáil, Charles Haughey. While many Irish people were either emigrating or struggling to make ends meet, Haughey lived like a lord in a mansion in north county Dublin. He spent tens of thousands of pounds a month on horses, wine, expensive clothes, the upkeep of an estate and the maintenance of a yacht. Much of the money for this lifestyle came from friends, associates and admirers who were themselves making huge amounts of money during the period.

Haughey and his associates and admirers had more than their wealth in common – many of them shared a financial advisor and accountant: the late Des Traynor.

Des Traynor was the first articled clerk in Haughey Boland, the accountancy firm which Charles Haughey founded in 1951. The two men were lifelong friends. Traynor looked after Haughey's finances. He sourced money for Haughey from rich business figures and hid this money from the Revenue. He ran a secret banking service from G&M which allowed many of these rich people to hide their money in the Cayman Islands, while at the same time being able to access their money by calling to see him at 17 College Green. He helped these people avoid and evade the taxes with which the rest of the population were being levied, often by Haughey-led governments. Des Traynor rose from an ordinary background to become one of the most respected businessmen of his generation, a multi-millionaire who, as often as not, spent his weekends in the then Taoiseach's home in Kinsealy. When he died in his sleep in 1994, the great and good of the Irish business world gathered to bid him farewell. Since then his reputation has been destroyed, and if he were alive today it is likely that he would be facing criminal charges.

The secret banking operation run by Traynor was, upon close examination, not as sophisticated as it at first appeared. It has been examined by the Moriarty Tribunal and by the Ansbacher inspectors who were appointed by the High Court in 1999 to report on what had been going on. In the course of these two inquiries quite startling anecdotes have emerged: tens of thousands of pounds being collected in cash from Guinness & Mahon for delivery to Charles Haughey; people handing over money in Dublin hotels and receiving no receipts; meetings over lunch in Dublin hotels where handwritten notes outlining the state of health of secret offshore accounts were distributed; a caretaker and a driver carrying boxes of cash around Dublin; and a secretary sitting at her desk counting this money before sending it on to its owners.

The Ansbacher inspectors, in their voluminous report published in 2002, identified 179 people and companies which were clients of Traynor's secret banking operation. Not all of those named in the inspectors' report are mentioned in this book. Some appear because of their closeness to Haughey, or because of the size of their business operations, or because they were active fund raisers for Fianna Fáil. Others are mentioned for human interest reasons, because they had some story to tell about Traynor or some observation to make about him. It is important to note that the fact that someone did business with Traynor and his offshore scheme does not automatically mean that that person did anything illegal. Many of those who set up Cayman accounts and Cayman trusts did so after receiving professional advice that it was legal to do so. Although the inspectors concluded that the offshore trust schemes run by Traynor were a sham, it would be wrong and unfair to conclude that everyone who set up such a trust was guilty of some wrongdoing. Futhermore, whilst the inspectors have made their own conclusions, the legality or otherwise of the Cayman trusts has never been tested in the courts.

On the other hand, it seems incontrovertible that Des Traynor operated a banking service without getting the required banking licence, that he organised matters so that his Cayman bank evaded the paying of Irish tax, and that he assisted others in evading tax. He lied to the Central Bank while acting as a director of a licenced Irish bank, and he secured money for Haughey and helped Haughey hide these payments from the Revenue. Why he did all of this we may never know. Greed and opportunity are one answer. The absence of any moral compass, with this being partly the product of the milieu in which he operated, is another. Unfortunately, Des Traynor is no longer around to give his side of the story.

What is beyond doubt, however, is that Des Traynor had an extraordinary capacity for discretion. People trusted him with their money and with the intimate details of their business and personal affairs. Charles Haughey trusted Traynor with the most sensitive and potentially devastating secret of his life and career – the truth behind his money. Traynor kept these and other secrets to himself and took them with him to his grave. Back in the basement of Number 17 College Green, however, the dust-covered microfiche records of Guinness & Mahon bank would be the beginning of his undoing.

Part One

The Ansbacher Deposits

1

The Old Boys Seek Out the New Boys

In 1965, a 31-year-old English man was sitting on a train on his way to his job with a firm of London stockbrokers. It was a damp, foggy morning and John Collins sat there looking gloomily out of the window and wondering what he was doing in such an awful country. He'd left school at 17 to work with the trustee department of Barclays bank in Luton, but had not been happy. He had taken time out for national service with the Royal Air Force, but despite wanting to, had not been posted overseas. After five years with the Luton bank and despite being promoted during that time, he decided he'd had enough. He left Barclays and got a job in the trustee department of the Nairobi branch of the National Bank of India. That was in 1957, when what are now called Kenya, Uganda and Tanzania were still joined under the banner of British East Africa. To be English and to have a position in a bank in Nairobi at the time meant a standard of living far above that which came with a comparable job back home. Also, the weather was an improvement on that of Luton and of England generally.

Collins was the number two in the trustee department of the Nairobi bank. The department acted as trustee and executor for clients, worked with wills, and managed the buying and selling of shares. Collins liked the work and the location. After about two or three years his senior left and Collins became the head of the department. However, the British empire was being dismantled and business in East Africa was tailing down for trustee executors. Most of the more wealthy people the bank acted for saw the way the wind was blowing and moved their assets, and themselves, out of Africa. In 1964 Collins left, returning to London where he got a job with a stock broking firm.

The weather got him down and that morning on the train gazing out at the London fog he decided he'd had enough. He looked at the job advertisements in the newspapers and noticed one for the Bank of Nova Scotia, in Jamaica. The location attracted him and he submitted an application. He was successful and was soon making his way to the Caribbean to take up the position of trust manager, Bank of Nova Scotia, Montego Bay. John Collins would spent the rest of his working life as a banker in the Caribbean.

Two hundred miles to the west of Montego Bay was a small trio of islands known as the Cayman Islands. The population was very small, a few thousand, and the economy, such as it was, was based on a bit of fishing and some tourism. The bulk of the small amount of land was low and marshy and there was no scope for agriculture. The islands had been noticed by Columbus on his way to the Americas, but he hadn't bothered stopping. They'd been popular at one time with pirates and the sea around the islands was scattered with underwater wrecks, some of which, it was said, had been carrying treasure when they sank. The capital, George Town, on the biggest island, Grand Cayman, was a typical sleepy Caribbean town with a harbour and single-storey clapboard houses with verandahs where you could sit in the evenings, sipping rum and looking out at the sky, the sea and the electrical storms.

The Montego Bay office of Bank of Nova Scotia began thinking about opening an office in the Cayman Islands. 'Cayman at that time, there was really nothing happening there but suffice to say that I used to go over there occasionally from Montego Bay,' Collins told the Ansbacher inspectors. 'In 1966, in July, I went over to Cayman to establish the office of the first resident trust company in Cayman in those days. I said: "It will only be a two years' hardship post". I stayed with the Nova Scotia Trust Company and we built up that company into a credible size.'

The initial operation was run by Collins, another banker, an accountant and a secretary. Some business did come their way and they were kept busy. Collins applied to the bank's regional headquarters in Nassau, in the Bahamas, for more help. They sent down a man six years Collins's junior, another English banker who wanted to make a career for himself in a warmer clime, John Furze. The two Englishmen were to become lifelong colleagues and friends.

Furze stayed in Cayman with Collins for about six months to help out and was then moved back to Barbados, to manage the Bank of Nova Scotia Trust Company office there. Business at the Cayman office continued to grow and Collins appealed for the return of Furze to help out. There was nothing much happening in Barbados and the bank agreed to Collins's request. When Furze came back to Cayman he took up the position of assistant manager. The two men set about growing their bank in what was then the fledgling Cayman Islands financial centre, but which would in time grow to become one of the largest in the world, with billions of dollars on deposit.

In the 1960s the manager of the Nova Scotia operation in Montego Bay was a man called Lyndsey Wellner. He and Collins became friends, but before long Wellner was posted to Dublin to open a Bank of Nova Scotia operation. According to Collins, when he set up his new bank in the Cayman Islands he began to travel touting for business. One of the places he went to was Dublin, where he met up with Wellner, who had made some key contacts in the local business community. Wellner introduced Collins to an Irish accountant, Des Traynor, an introduction which was to become a key moment in Collins's professional career.

Traynor was a senior partner and tax expert with the accountancy firm Haughey Boland and acted as an advisor to many of the wealthy Irish people who would be of interest to the offshore trust and banking operation Collins was busy setting up. Traynor had been the first articled apprentice taken on by the Haughey Boland firm after it was set up in 1951, and he had been articled to its more famous partner, Charles Haughey. Haughey himself was a prize-winning accountancy student who had graduated with first class honours in Commerce from University College, Dublin. Haughey's main role in the firm was to bring in clients and his true interest lay more in a career in politics than a career in accountancy. As he pursued his political ambitions, Haughey became more and more detached from his accountancy firm. Traynor, on the other hand, was a workaholic who became the main force behind the firm and a key factor in its early growth.

Des Traynor was bright, sharp, and ambitious. He prospered as an accountant and, later, as a top corporate executive, because of his huge capacity for work, his love of complex financial and corporate structures, and his drive. He could quickly absorb convoluted detail, had a prodigious memory, and was discreet to a degree which was unusual even for accountants and bankers. People placed enormous trust in him and for the most part he never let them down. Cautious, secretive and avaricious people trusted him not only with the most sensitive details of their business affairs – they also trusted him with their money.

Traynor was six years younger than Haughey, and at five-feet six-inches he was also smaller than the diminutive Haughey. He liked sports and was a soccer fan. One former associate said of him that he got as excited about a tax scheme as he did about a soccer match. He was overweight and this, together with his workrate, may have contributed to early heart trouble. He was a teetotaler who loved dinner parties and social gatherings generally. The large house he and his family lived in was architect-designed so that Traynor could host large *soirées*. You walked in the main door and there was a huge reception hall with a chandelier hanging from the ceiling.

Traynor's family was important to him and he made time for them. He organised an offshore trust for his family and did the same for friends and neighbours. Many of his friends' children now find themselves dealing with tax issues concerning their inheritances, going back decades and involving public scrutiny.

A significant aspect of Traynor's working life was assisting the avoidance if not the evasion of tax. As taxes on capital were introduced and developed in the Irish Republic from the 1970s on, Traynor sought to assist his rich friends and clients in protecting their money from this threat to their wealth. Whatever his intentions – and they seem pretty clear by now – the secret structures he put in place were open to being used by people wishing to criminally evade paying their proper taxes. This is a general point which could be applied to most of the State's main financial institutions, with their networks of banks in offshore locations, but Traynor's case is arguably different because of the extraordinary level of clandestine activity involved and because of some of the clients for whom he acted. Most notable of all, of course, is Haughey, the leading political figure of the period. Haughey was the champion of the sort of business developments pursued by many of the people who were clients of Traynor. Some of these clients gave money to Haughey himself, while others were major financial supporters of Haughey's party, Fianna Fáil. These connections and friendships fuelled allegations that a golden circle existed at the heart of Irish business life. These allegations were not without some basis.

Traynor was a great accountant and business advisor generally. He was praised for the quality of his advice and for his calmness under pressure. He played a key role in the creation and development of Cement Roadstone Holdings, perhaps the greatest success to date in the Irish business world.

He was considered to be a 'blue chip' businessman. The Ansbacher inspectors said of him: 'Mr Traynor appears to have been a man of formidable capabilities, who went on to become one of the outstanding financiers of the 1980s and 1990s. He was reserved to the point of taciturnity; a man who could truly be said not to have permitted his left hand to know what his right hand was doing. At the same time he was, according to his secretary, a man devoted to his family who, no matter how pressing his business engagements, would never miss a family holiday. He was also a man who inspired absolute trust and confidence in all who met him.'

The successful property developer and businessman, John Byrne, told the inspectors of his first meeting with Traynor. It was around 1960 when Traynor went down to Tralee, Co. Kerry, to do an audit on the Brandon Hotel, which was owned by Byrne together with Thomas and William Clifford. Traynor was accompanied by another Haughey Boland accountant, Jack Stakelum. 'They came down to do the audit some time in the afternoon and they worked all night. I said I would see them in the morning and they were gone. They finished the whole lot. They worked all night and they were gone back to Dublin... So I said, "God, these are some characters." And after that I became very friendly with him... Anything I did I consulted with him... He was a remarkable fellow.'

Byrne also said of Traynor: 'He was the sort of man, it doesn't matter what sort of problem you had or worry you had. He had the capacity of saying, "Well, what are you worrying about? It's nothing. I can solve that." He was like that.'

By the time Collins met up with Traynor during his trip to Dublin in the late 1960s, Traynor was not only a key player in many of the major business deals going on then, he was also a key link man to Haughey and the political forces behind the economic changes underway in Dublin. He was just the sort of man Collins needed to meet.

Collins made a number of trips to Dublin. The Irish economy was experiencing a boom after it had been opened up to international trade by Seán Lemass. There was a lot of building development in particular, with large amounts of money being made through property deals and house-building. 'Everyone was in Ireland at the time, the Royal Trust and everyone else, looking for business. We were almost the last man on the block coming in,' Collins said. During one of Collins's trips to Ireland, Lydnsey Wellner brought him to meet John Guinness in Guinness & Mahon bank on College Green.

Collins and Guinness may have first met when Guinness was in the Cayman Islands. According to William Forwood, another senior executive in G&M at the time: 'John Guinness was very much a sailing man and my recollection is that he went on a sailing holiday in the Cayman Islands. While he was there he was offered land. Anyway there was land available which was thought to be ripe for development. When he came back he discussed this with his cousin, James Guinness, and it was decided to form a little company to buy some land with a view to development.'

In June 1969, Collins called to see Sir George Mahon and John Guinness at the Dublin bank. Liam McGonagle, a solicitor and entrepreneur who gave legal advice to the bank and also used it in his business dealings, was present.

Collins was back in Dublin again in October 1969. A G&M memo recorded: 'Collins of Nova Scotia Trust Company has put up to us a proposition involving a loan to purchase 150 acres in the Cayman Islands for $200,000. We are offered 9 per cent on the loan and a minimum of 25 per cent of the equity. It has been agreed that JR shall fly out to investigate this project at once.' JR was an official in G&M.

A syndicate involving G&M directors and directors from its parent in London was put together for the deal. Forwood, in his interview with the Ansbacher inspectors in July 2001, said the deal did not make money. 'I think there are still some properties there,' he added.

Guinness & Mahon bank had been established in 1836 by John Ross Mahon and Robert Guinness, both members of prominent and wealthy Anglo-Irish families. Robert Guinness was a relative of the Guinness brewing family, whose stout brewing operation in St James's Gate, Dublin, grew to become one of the most successful drinks companies in the world. John Ross Mahon's family came from Ahascragh, Co.Galway, where the Mahons had an estate going back a number of generations.

The bank acted as a land agent for estates around the country and for many years this work, involved managing estates and collecting rents, was its main source of income. Mahon acted as land agent for his namesake (but not a relative), Major Mahon, from Strokestown, Co. Roscommon, the landlord who was murdered during the famine and whose home is now a famine museum. He also acted for Castlegar, his family estate in Galway.

G&M did well and in time opened a sub-office in London. In 1923, following the War of Independence and the succession of the Free State from the United Kingdom, the Dublin and London banks swapped roles, with London becoming the head office and Dublin becoming a branch. The bank's name appeared in the prospectus for the first National Loan raised by the Free State in 1923.

One of the sources of income the bank had was looking after trusts established by members of the wealthy Guinness family. The bank established operations in the Channel Islands which managed trusts set up there. As the Irish Republic was in the sterling area there was no difficulty with this. Although they withdrew from politics, much of 20th century commercial life in Dublin was dominated by Protestants, and G&M's customers were almost exclusively Protestant.

Throughout the 1900s the bank managed to maintain representatives of the two founding families on the board. By the late 1960s G&M was being run by a three-member group, known as the 'conclave'. The three men, all bearing the title managing director, were John Guinness, Sir George Mahon and William Forwood. Forwood described the set up: 'It was a very old-fashioned and very small affair. The directors sat together in what was known as the Partners Room... We all sat in the same room. We discussed approaches made to us to borrow funds.' Such a set up was not unusual in London at the time, he added.

By now the bank wasn't doing all that well and the three men recognised that they needed to do something about the leisurely, old-fashioned style with which they were overseeing their business. The three were the products of the same privileged Protestant background and had even been to the same school. Meanwhile, outside the walls of the College Green premises, the Free State had become the Irish Republic and, following the reversal of its isolationist economic policies under the government of Lemass, its economy was on something of a roll. There was a lot of building going on, new housing estates on the edges of the city, old city-centre Georgian buildings being knocked down to make way for office blocks to house the swelling ranks of the Civil Service. There was money to be made, but most of the money was being made by people who were a million miles away from the 'old boys' privileged background that the three bankers belonged to. Something needed to be done about this, the bankers decided.

They had another idea, too. Following the meetings with Collins, the men thought that they might be able to make money using the Cayman Islands as part of their banking operations. In January 1969, at a meeting of the conclave, the three decided to look at forming a company or trust in the Cayman Islands or some other tax haven. This would look after the investment they were making on the islands, but it might also, if the Cayman executive council allowed, begin to operate as a bank.

When Charles Haughey graduated from University College Dublin in the late 1940s he was a strong supporter of Fianna Fáil, and doing a line with Maureen Lemass, daughter of Seán Lemass, whom he'd started to date while the two were in university. Harry Boland, with whom he went into business, was a Fianna Fáil blue-blood. His father, Gerry, served as Minister for Justice in the period between 1932 and 1948. In time, his brother would also become a government minister.

Haughey, a scholarship boy from north Dublin who was, like Traynor, educated by the Christian Brothers, was able, ambitious and well connected. He wanted to be rich but he didn't wish to spend his life working as an accountant. Politics attracted him, and he hoped to become Taoiseach one day, but he wouldn't let all this prevent him from enjoying a lavish lifestyle. He wanted, as a friend would say many years later, 'to travel first class'.

Des Traynor, however, was not very interested in politics and one wonders why he chose to get involved in helping Haughey in the way that he did. The obvious answer is that it was simply a relationship which evolved, and that he admired Haughey and wished to play some role in the transformation of the Irish economy and Haughey's modernising work generally. However, Traynor's link with Haughey was a key element in Traynor's business career, as many of his major clients were people who were with Haughey Boland because of its links with Haughey and Fianna Fáil. Traynor's links through Haughey to this new strand of Irish economic life increased his attractiveness to the G&M conclave.

Bringing clients to his new firm was a key part of Haughey's work in the 1950s. While working as an accountant he was also pursuing his political career, taking up positions in the Fianna Fáil organisation and seeking election to the Dáil. He first stood for Dublin North-East in 1951 but was unsuccessful. He tried again in 1954 and again in a by-election in 1956. In March 1957 he was at last successful, getting elected to the Dáil for the first time in the last general election of the pre-television age. When the Dáil re-convened, Eamon de Valera, then 75 years old, was elected Taoiseach for what was going to be his last term.

Haughey was very much associated with the need for economic development and the embracing of capitalism. He had married Maureen Lemass in 1951. Her father, as Minister for Industry and Commerce, had come into contact with many of the people who were to prosper in Ireland over the coming decades. These included P V Doyle, Matt Gallagher and John Byrne. Haughey, too, came to know these people and they became clients of his fledgling account-ancy firm. The firm was obviously close to Fianna Fáil and many of its clients were financial supporters of the party. Later, some of these people would become members of the controversial party fund-raising group, Taca. Haughey was very involved with the group, as was his partner in the firm, Harry Boland. There was a seamlessness about the whole scenario.

Lemass, when he replaced De Valera, urged Irish businessmen to embrace the new economic policy, one which saw the creation of wealth by businessmen as playing a key role in the development of the state, the ending of poverty and of chronic emigration. Able, aggressive businessmen, seeking profits, would be the salvation of the Republic. Byrne, who had built a successful business for himself in Britain run-ning dance halls used by Irish emigrants, was one of those encouraged by Lemass to come back to Ireland and take part in the new adventure. Haughey was a key political contact and representative for many of these men. Traynor, much more discreetly, was their problem solver and financial adviser. There was little or no dividing line between business and politics. Economic growth was the key political project of the day.

In the course of the 1950s, Haughey became a significant figure on the national stage. After marrying the Taoiseach's daughter, he and his new wife set up home in a semi-detached house on the Howth Road in Dublin. Haughey grew his business and got elected to the Dáil. In 1961, the leader of Fine Gael, John Dillon, praised his 'exceptional and outstanding ability'.

Haughey was an unabashed supporter of the benefits of capitalism, materialism and the desire to make money. In his maiden speech to the Dáil in May 1957, he said: 'I would like to put forward the proposition that what is wrong with this country is that too many people are making insufficient profits... the problem is not that our bloated industrialists make too much profit, but that too few of our industrialists are able to carry on at all.' The profit motive would fuel economic development, he argued. This was at odds with the views held by many of the older members of the party.

Haughey retired as an active partner in Haughey Boland after he was appointed to the post of parliamentary secretary to the Minister for Justice, Oscar Traynor (no relation to Des), in May 1960. He retained his 25 per cent interest in Haughey Boland, as a partner, but within a short time he was no longer taking any salary or income from it. This, however, did not prevent him from becoming more and more asset rich.

In the October 1961 general election he topped the poll in his constituency and was subsequently appointed Minister for Justice. The following year he became the first member of cabinet to own a race horse when he acquired a five-year-old bay mare called Miss Cossie. Some of the older and more republican members of Fianna Fáil did not approve of this flashiness. They regarded the Mercedes and Jaguar cars, hunts and racehorses, as the trappings of the old, disliked, ascendancy. Haughey, on the other hand, wanted to not just ape the ascendancy, he wanted to become part of it.

A picture of how Traynor's career at the Haughey Boland firm was developing during this period was given by the accountant, Jack Stakelum, in his evidence to the Ansbacher inspectors. Stakelum, who described Traynor as one of his closest friends, worked as an articled clerk with Haughey Boland from 1956 to 1958.

'It was a relatively small practice. There was just Charlie Haughey and Harry Boland, the two partners. Des Traynor would have been manager. He would have been shortly qualified, around 1955/1956. There were maybe six to eight articled clerks. I think there were four each allowed, I am not too sure. A couple of secretaries; mostly auditing work.'

Stakelum worked closely with Traynor. He left to work with another firm, but returned to Haughey Boland in 1962 as a qualified accountant. By this time Traynor was a partner. Again, Stakelum worked closely with Traynor, with the relationship this time being that of a partner and a manager, as opposed to a manager and a junior. 'I think I would have been displacing him from a lot of situations. He would have been moving on to other things... he was almost severing himself from the normal auditing work.

'When I say that he moved on to other things he certainly seemed to extricate himself a lot from the day-to-day work. He was a workaholic so it wasn't a question of not working but there were things that he got involved in. He got involved with clients in a very big way. He was certainly with a company called Merchant Banking (part of the Gallagher group) and he would have, at least every Friday morning, always been at a board meeting there. I don't know if he was on the board now, but he was always at a board meeting there and he would get involved in other situations... I know that before he left to join Guinness & Mahon he got very involved with projects that they were involved with, property projects that the bank were involved in, he was in an advisory capacity.'

The Gallagher group was a Haughey Boland client with which Traynor was very involved. 'Matt Gallagher would have been the owner of it and there were groups of building companies there, I'm not sure what they would have been but he would have been very involved with that.' At the time, Matt Gallagher was giving one day a month to Taca fund-raising business.

Stakelum said that Traynor was 'very brilliant on a cross section of work'. Companies Office files show that Traynor became a member of the board of the main Gallagher group companies in 1961. The group was at the time a huge building and property development operation headed by Matt Gallagher, a Fianna Fáil supporter and friend of Charles Haughey. By 1961, Traynor, a partner with Haughey Boland, was living in a house in a development built by the Gallaghers, at 12 Raheny Park, Howth Road, not far from Neil Blaney TD, who also had a home in the Gallagher development. Later in the 1960s, the Gallagher company shares were assigned to Gallagher Trusts Ltd. In April 1972, the shares were transferred to a holding company in the Cayman Islands, Bering Estates Ltd. Its address was at the Bank of Nova Scotia Trust Company, where Collins and Furze were working.

In 1961, the year Traynor and Christopher Gore-Grimes joined the board of Gallagher Group Ltd, the two men also joined the board of Carlisle Trust Ltd, a company owned by another property developer and Haughey supporter, John Byrne. (The Gore-Grimes family came from Howth, just like John Guinness, were avid sailors, and were members of the Howth Yacht Club, the club Haughey would later join.) In July 1972 the bulk of the Carlisle Trust shares were transferred to the Cayman Islands.

Both of the property developers, Gallagher and Byrne, were friends of Charles Haughey, and significant business figures in their day. They were important clients for both Haughey Boland and for Traynor. Another significant business figure and friend of Haughey's to whom Traynor became a valued advisor was the hotelier, Pascal Vincent Doyle, the force behind the development of the Doyle hotel chain, which included the Berkeley Court, Tara Towers and Burlington Hotel in Dublin.

In his dealings with heavy-hitter property developers Traynor worked closely with G&M and made an impression. Matters developed and as the 1960s drew to a close the conclave decided that Traynor was the man they needed to bring new business to their bank. They decided to ask him to come on board as a senior executive, in essence to join the conclave. The move would involve him leaving Haughey Boland. The suggestion was put to him, Traynor said he'd think about it, and in the end he agreed. It was a major move for him as he had spent almost twenty years, and all his working life, with the firm. However, he had outgrown Haughey Boland and it was time for him to move on.

'I think the word would be shock,' Stakelum said, when asked about how the move was received in Haughey Boland. 'Because he would have been, he was a workaholic, he would have worked morning, noon and night. He would have been a real corner stone of the partnership and he would have been considered a massive loss to a relatively struggling partnership. That's why it would have been a shock.'

Stakelum said that Traynor would have given his fellow partners a few months' notice. 'But prior to that he would have been substantially involved with work connected with Guinness & Mahon. He used to be with them far more than he was with us at Haughey Boland at the time... He worked with them on some property schemes and taxation schemes... He obviously made a very able contribution to whatever they were doing because they invited him to join the board in a very senior capacity there... I think he was keeping his end up in Haughey Boland as well, working nights and weekends.'

Forwood gave his account to the inspectors as to how the appointment came about. 'We were conscious, when I say we I mean George Mahon and John Guinness and I, that we all came from the same background. We were all educated in the same school. We were all Protestants. None of us really had, we thought, sufficient connection with the wider world and we were very anxious to expand, and we were very much tarred with the Protestant brush, let's face it; our clients, our employees. We wanted to change this and we decided there was room for another. We debated this for a long time and we had come across, all of us had come across, Mr Traynor... We all knew him for business reasons.

'We, the three of us talking together, wrote out a specification, a kind of thing we were looking for, and somebody said this could be Traynor, and we approached him. He had recently had a very serious heart attack and I can remember him saying: "Give me until tomorrow to decide whether to tell my wife. If I tell my wife I shall accept because she will make me." Anyway he did tell his wife and he joined us.'

2

The Offshore Bank on College Green

WHEN Des Traynor took up his position in the Partners Parlour of G&M as co-managing director on 11 December 1969, the bank was already busy setting up its links with the Cayman Islands, and Traynor was well-informed as to developments. He hit the ground running. He had the experience of being on the board of Merchant Banking. As a former partner in an accountancy firm and close adviser to some of the most successful business figures in the state, he knew exactly what these people's banking requirements were. He quickly set about taking charge of supplying a service to meet their needs.

The story goes that at his first board meeting he was slightly uncomfortable when he found himself surrounded by men who all came from a background which was very different from his. The others were all public school graduates, some flew in from London for the meeting, one or two were titled. When the tea trolley was brought in, Traynor was offered Indian or China. Traynor selected Indian then sat while everyone else selected China.

But the differences were all on the surface. Traynor, like his colleagues in the bank, was interested in business and making profits. He did not underestimate his own talents, and the bank had taken him on because it recognised them as well. He was a tough, hard-working man who liked to get on with it. Forwood had this to say of him: 'Mr Traynor was a very dominant personality... He was rather inclined to do his own thing, perhaps with less consultation than others of us would have thought desirable. You know this is not intended as a criticism of him, but perhaps that is so.'

In June 1970, Traynor returned from a meeting in Guinness & Mahon's London headquarters and reported to his colleagues in Dublin about the incorporation of a bank in the Cayman Islands. It would be called Guinness Mahon Cayman Trust (GMCT). A memo from 19 July 1970 showed the matter progressing. The Executive Council in the Cayman Islands had approved in principle the application from GMCT for a banking licence. According to Forwood, it was John Collins and his partner in the Bank of Nova Scotia, John Furze, who put it to G&M that it should form a bank in Cayman. It was part of their idea that they would leave Bank of Nova Scotia to work full time in GMCT and would have a shareholding in it. 'I am fairly certain that the initiative came from them,' said Forwood. The Dublin board agreed to the proposal. It thought Furze and Collins would have some useful connections and might be able to attract deposits from overseas, particularly from the United States.

Furze and Collins were to each own approximately 20 per cent of the new bank, with the Dublin bank owning the rest. 'The object of the exercise was that these two young men had left the Bank of Nova Scotia and were going to play an important part in the development of the bank in Cayman and it would be as well to tie them in.'

By 1972 the new bank had a limited licence to trade and by 1974 it had a full banking licence under Cayman law. Around this time Collins and Furze took over management of the bank. Traynor was the bank's chairman. The bank took deposits from expatriate US citizens living in the Caribbean area. It also began to do business with Dublin at an early date.

As well as setting up a Cayman bank to take deposits, G&M was also involved in setting up a trust management service. As early as May 1971, meetings were taking place in Dublin between Traynor, Collins and representatives of the successful Dublin accountancy firm,

Kennedy Crowley. These meetings were 'the genesis of a mutually profitable liaison between Kennedy Crowley and Guinness & Mahon', the inspectors later reported.

A memo from February 1972 recorded that Traynor and Furze had had a number of meetings with Kennedy Crowley. 'There have been a number of enquiries about setting up discretionary settlements.' Discretionary trusts are trusts where the assets are handed over so that they are managed by the trustees, at their, the trustees' discretion. In this way the assets pass into the control and, in ways, the ownership of another entity. This has certain tax advantages. At the end of the period for which the trust is to exist, the accumulated assets are then distributed by the trustees to the beneficiaries of the trust. What GMCT was offering was a service whereby the Cayman bank would manage such trusts, a service that would also involve the provision of trustees. The system which the bank developed in this regard involved an extraordinary level of secrecy, though the bank was not unique in this.

In their report the inspectors said: 'To understand the background to the discretionary trust schemes operated by GMCT, one must return to the early 1970s. In that era, personal tax rates were high and the political preparations were underway to introduce capital taxes such as Capital Gains, Capital Acquisitions and Wealth Taxes. In these conditions, those with money were concerned about their financial future and were receptive to schemes that appeared to offer a measure of security.

'The class of person with these concerns was also, coincidentally, the target market of Guinness & Mahon, who wished to provide personal banking services to wealthy clients. The major accountancy firms in Dublin at that time were developing tax strategies to respond to their clients' concerns. Guinness & Mahon facilitated this development by providing vehicles to implement such schemes. It was a common feature of such schemes that those wishing to avail of them wanted to locate their assets in tax havens.'

In the early 1970s the tax regime was very different to what it is now. Income tax was levied at 35 per cent with a series of surtaxes for incomes above £2,500. The highest surtax rate was 45 per cent. There were no taxes on gains from the sale of capital; in other words, no taxes on profits from transactions involving land, property, the sale of companies, and so on. In 1974 the income tax rate was changed and a new scale of rates introduced. The lowest rate was 26 per cent and it rose, via four more rates, to 80 per cent for all income over £8,350. In other words, for every £1 earned at the top rate, the earner got 20p and the State got 80p.

This cripplingly high rate was reduced to 60 per cent by the end of the 1970s. Through the 1980s the high income tax rates continued. In the 1981/1982 tax year, when Haughey was in power, the top income tax rate was 60 per cent. In 1988/1989, when Haughey was back in power, the top rate was 58 per cent. These rates created a strong temptation to evade income tax, a temptation which a significant proportion of the non-PAYE population found impossible to resist.

The introduction by the Labour/Fine Gael coalition government of taxes on capital for the first time in 1975 was something which caused concern to a more limited range of people. The new taxes applied to the 1974/1975 tax year and their introduction led to the then Minister for Finance, Richie Ryan, being dubbed 'Red Richie'. Capital Gains Tax, a tax on profits from the purchase and sale of assets, was introduced at a rate of 26 per cent. In other words, if a property speculator made £100,000 from the purchase and sale of a building, he could keep all his profits in 1973, but only three-quarters of them in 1974. The introduction of the tax made a lot of rich people turn against Fine Gael.

A year later, Capital Acquisitions Tax, a tax on gifts and inheritances, was introduced and back-dated to the 1974/1975 tax year. The rates varied according to the circumstances, and ranged from zero to 60 per cent. A further levy on the more well-to-do sections of society was introduced in 1975, a wealth tax. This was a 1 per cent levy on the assets of well-off people, with the family home being omitted from the calculation of the value of the assets. The tax remained in place for three years.

These taxes created great concern, if not outrage and consternation, among the more well-off sections of society, and formed the back-drop to much of what happened in the early 1970s in G&M. The new taxes created two impulses: the impulse to seek to have the taxes abolished; and the impulse to avoid or evade them. It was in respect of the latter impulse that people sought out Des Traynor and G&M.

Traynor began to build a system whereby people in the Republic could move their money offshore, safe from the clutches of 'Red Richie'. Often the money was taken in cash to London, where it was handed over and then moved offshore. Suitcases of money were handed over in London hotel rooms.

As the 1970s progressed and the Cayman Islands split from the sterling area and then, later, the Republic split from sterling, exchange control issues arose. Exchange control was a law which stipulated that money could not be moved in and out of the sterling area, and later the Irish State, without permission. In Ireland the authority to oversee the law was delegated by the Central Bank to the commercial banks. Traynor managed to circumvent these laws and the G&M offshore deposits continued to grow.

Sometimes money was simply placed on deposit, offshore, in the name of the depositor. In other instances, the money given to Traynor was placed in a – nominally – discretionary trust. The trustees, the off-shore bank, would then manage the money, often by simply leaving it on deposit. Sometimes, the trust would in turn own a company, a registered name with no real business activity, and the funds might be placed on deposit in the name of this company. On occasion the trust might be in the Channel Islands and the company in the Cayman Islands. In general, trusts were established when there were larger amounts of money involved and when the depositor wanted to put some money away for his or her children.

The Ansbacher inspectors decided in their report that much of the trust structure put in place by Traynor was a 'sham'. This was princi-pally because Traynor offered a service where in reality, if not in law, the persons who handed over their money to him retained control of that money. Not only that, but they were offered direct access to the money by way of Traynor. To achieve this, Traynor had some of the offshore money re-deposited back in Dublin, in G&M, under the name of the offshore bank concerned. The money would be placed on deposit in, for instance, the name of GMCT.

In GMCT the books of that bank would show Joe Bloggs having £10,000 on deposit. If Bloggs then, in Dublin, asked Traynor for £5,000, Traynor would withdraw the money from the GMCT account in G&M and hand it to Bloggs. He would inform the Cayman bank which would then enter a withdrawal from the Bloggs account there. In other words, in the G&M books you would see a withdrawal of £5,000 from the GMCT account, but in the Cayman books you would see a withdrawal of £5,000 from the Joe Bloggs account. The GMCT account in Dublin might contain millions of pounds and would represent the money owned by a number of individuals and trusts.

Often the money never went to the Cayman Islands at all. The books of the Dublin bank would make it look like it had because the money was in an account in Dublin in the name of the Cayman bank. In these cases the money was lodged, left on deposit, and withdrawn from the Dublin bank, without ever going to the Cayman Islands. It was often a simple legal fiction. The 'offshore' money was, in fact, held in a bank which was literally across the road from the Irish Central Bank.

Customers were offered this service in a discreet way. Most of the customers were people who had dealings in some way or another with Traynor or the bank. Some were people who went looking for advice from Kennedy Crowley. The customers would be told the bank could 'look after' their money. In some cases the depositor knew where the money would be kept. In other cases the depositor was not too clear about exactly what was happening.

In 1974 Furze and Collins moved from Bank of Nova Scotia to take up the positions of full-time joint managers with Guinness Mahon Cayman Trust. Collins concentrated on business from North America and Furze concentrated on the Irish business. Furze would travel to Dublin a number of times a year to reconcile his Cayman books with accounts kept in Dublin by Traynor. On occasion he would meet with prospective customers of his Cayman bank and tout for business. It was in this way that there came into existence a document called 'A Note to John Furze'.

The note was written in the wake of a September 1983 meeting between Furze and a Dublin businessman, Ray McLoughlin. The meeting was arranged by Traynor and held in G&M. The note was written by McLoughlin and outlined some key aspects of the trust structures which Traynor and his colleagues had put in place during the 1970s as their offshore/onshore banking service developed. As it is based on what Furze presented to McLoughlin, it gives a good account of what people were being offered and of Furze and Traynor's views on the system that had been developed by them during the 1970s. What emerges from the document is the fact that the chief concern of the bankers and customers involved was that the Irish authorities would never learn of the existence of the money lodged with the Cayman bank. In order not to arouse their suspicions, it was necessary that the whole structure created by Traynor during the 1970s be hidden from the authorities. The document is almost exclusively concerned with the issue of secrecy. Although the descriptions have to do with trusts, the overall conspiratorial aspect of what is described can be taken as applying also to simple cash deposits.

Discretionary trusts are trusts to which assets are given with the trustees having discretion over what happens to the assets while they are controlled by the trust. When the trust is disbursed, it goes to the beneficiaries nominated by the person who established the trust. The service offered by Furze and Traynor seems to have been designed so that the trusts would never be discovered, even after the assets held by the trusts had been disbursed to beneficiaries.

According to the note drafted by McLoughlin, 'maximum flexibility' in relation to who could be a beneficiary of a trust could be achieved by 'the beneficiaries under the trust being specified as anybody, whether corporate or individual, who would subscribe $10 to the Red Cross and would be able to deliver a certificate of subscription to the Trustees.' In other words, the beneficiaries' names would not have to be stated, but the assets could still be distributed when the time came simply by the intended beneficiaries making the (very small) contribution to the Red Cross. According to the note '*noms de plume*' could also be used when specifying beneficiaries.

The trustees – the persons managing the funds – in practice did nothing with the assets they held without being told to do so by the person who established the trust, according to the note. 'Clients do not like communicating instructions to the trustees by paper and therefore it is quite usual that instructions would be given by phone. Telephonic recognition of the client's voice by an executive operating for the trustees would ordinarily be sufficient, but if it were somebody who was not known to some executive of the trustees then he might be asked to name an identification number or perhaps to give his own passport number... In any case there probably would be some conduit between the client and the trustees such as Mr X (1), for example, in the case of GMCT.' Mr X (1) was Des Traynor.

A rather bizarre example of how someone might be given money from a trust was given in the note. 'If the client wants Billy Bloggs to have $10,000 in a bank account in the south of France, the trustees would settle that amount in X Ltd which would be the beneficiary in the list of beneficiaries on the trust deed. X Ltd would then transfer the funds to whatever account it wished. The money has not been settled on B Bloggs and therefore the operation of the trust is not in breach of any law. What might happen then is that X Ltd might engage Bloggs for a job in the south of France and pay him $10,000 for doing that job. If Bloggs were an Irish resident and if he did not declare receipt of the money and bring it back he would be in breach of taxation and exchange control.' Elsewhere in the note it was stated that this method of getting money out of the trust could be used to get money to anyone the client liked.

What happened after the client died was also examined. At one point it was stated that beneficiaries of the trust might see the list of beneficiaries after the client's death. 'It would be important therefore to leave out mistresses and such like.'

Secrecy was the recurring theme. Only very senior officers in GMCT would know the details of a particular trust, according to the note. The only parties who would know about an Irish resident's trust would be: 'X1, X2, JF and perhaps 3 or 4 of his officers.' This is a reference to Traynor, another Dublin banker, Furze and three or four GMCT executives. 'The making of arrangements with the trustees with regard to the disposition of funds in the case of the death of a client can be given effect to without going through a will which must be probated and would be a public document.

'Nobody in Dublin other than the two principals would know about any trust arrangement and there would be no record of any kind anywhere in Dublin or any reference in any correspondence between GMCT and Dublin in relation to any trust arrangement.

'There are no duplicate copies of trust documents anywhere outside of GMCT. Consideration is being given to having a set of duplicate copies somewhere but no decision has been reached on it.'

A summary of three benefits of a discretionary trust were listed. They were: money could be moved simply by a phone call to a contact operating for the trustees; if the client died the trust money could be passed on according to the client's wishes, but without the use of a will which would come to the attention of the Revenue; and because all assets in a discretionary trust were legally not controlled or owned by the client, the client was not in breach of exchange control regulations. 'The bank in Ireland (G&M) can swear to the Revenue as to the non-connection in the legal sense between any parties it might be inquiring about, and any legal trust.'

McLoughlin told the Moriarty Tribunal that he gave some consideration to opening such a trust, but in the end did not. He told the inspectors that he negotiated a loan from G&M in 1984 on behalf of his brother, Colm, who was a resident of Dubai, in the Arab Emirates. The loan was given using a GMCT company called Selima. Colm McLoughlin swore an affidavit to the inspectors in which he stated that the loan was his, and the inspectors accepted that evidence.

In time, the Cayman bank was sold to the Henry Ansbacher group and renamed Ansbacher Cayman Ltd. It was for this reason that the whole scheme put together by Traynor during the 1970s was later dubbed the Ansbacher Deposits. Although Ansbacher had nothing to do with the scheme in the 1970s and for most of the 1980s, the term Ansbacher Deposits was nevertheless used to describe the structure put in place by Traynor when it was discovered.

An aspect of the Ansbacher structure was that people in Ireland were essentially treating G&M as a branch of the Cayman bank. Customers could lodge money to their 'offshore' account through College Green and could make withdrawals from their 'offshore account' through College Green. All the time that their money was on deposit, it might remain in College Green. A complicated legal and banking scenario, something which amounted to an elaborate fiction, was put in place to support this service.

The Dublin bank needed to keep track of who was depositing money and who was withdrawing money, but it did not want to keep accounts on its books which would track these movements. To do so would allow the Central Bank to spot what was going on when it, the Central Bank, conducted one of its regular, on-site inspections of the bank. Likewise, having accounts on its books in the names of the actual clients would create the risk that the Revenue might discover the accounts. A way around this was developed by Traynor and the bank. They began to operate something called 'memorandum accounts'.

The memorandum accounts tracked who owned the money which was on deposit in G&M in the name of GMCT. The memorandum accounts were not on the books of G&M. On the bank's books it would look as if, for example, £3 million was being held on deposit in one account by GMCT. In fact, this would be money owned by a number of different Irish customers. If Joe Bloggs called into Traynor and gave him £10,000 to put into this account, Traynor would lodge the money, and the bank's books would show the Cayman bank's account growing by £10,000. Meanwhile, Traynor would go to the memorandum accounts and make an entry to Joe Bloggs' memorandum account, crediting it with £10,000. A search through the memorandum accounts would allow all the money held in the Cayman bank's accounts in G&M to be attributed to the various Irish customers.

These memorandum accounts were secret, and their existence was not to be revealed to the Central Bank. It was through his work with these accounts that a bank official, Pádraig Collery, was to become involved in the operation of the Ansbacher Deposits.

Collery, from Sligo, started his banking career with Lloyds Bank in London in 1968. He moved to Dublin in 1974 to start as a senior official in G&M. Among the duties Collery took on was responsibility for the Dublin bank's computer system. Within a short time Traynor took Collery into his confidence in relation to the memorandum accounts, and Collery began to take instructions from Traynor in relation to the making of entries to the accounts. The accounts were kept on the G&M computer system, but in an area of the system which could only be accessed by people who had the required password. This type of restricted area of a computer system is called a bureau system and it was by accessing the bureau system that Collery made the entries he was requested to make by his boss, Traynor.

The large deposit accounts kept by GMCT in G&M were referred to later as the pooled accounts. These pooled accounts were sterling accounts and the memorandum accounts maintained by Traynor and Collery were also sterling accounts. Other amounts in different currencies also appeared on the G&M books in the name of GMCT, but in these cases the amounts in each account were the property of individual Irish customers. The currencies most used were US and Australian dollars, and Deutschmarks.

There was a further layer of secrecy to the whole affair. The memorandum accounts were not kept in the names of their owners, but were given codes. Traynor knew who lay behind each code. Accounts coded S8 and S9, for instance, belonged to Haughey. In time, Collery got to know who lay behind many of the codes as did Traynor's long-standing secretary, Joan Williams. Collery did this work with the memorandum accounts as part of his G&M duties and received no remuneration for it. He also, every month or so, oversaw the issuing of GMCT bank statements to the customers who had 'offshore' accounts through Traynor. Collery would source the GMCT stationery from a cupboard in G&M, use it to replace the G&M

stationery in the bank's printers, and then oversee the printing by G&M staff of GMCT bank statements which would be later issued to the Irish customers. Copies of the statements would be sent to Cayman. The statements sent to the customers would have the name GMCT cut off before they were put in the post.

A further element to the structure was also established. Sam Field-Corbett was a friend of Traynor's who had worked with him in Haughey Boland. Field-Corbett was involved in supplying secretarial services to clients of Haughey Boland. Company secretarial services is a specialist area involving the creation and supply of registered companies, the maintenance of share registers, the filing of accounts and so on. In the mid-1970s, Field-Corbett, with Traynor's encouragement, left Haughey Boland and established his own company, Management Investment Services. Traynor said he'd send business in Field-Corbett's direction, and he proved good to his word. Field-Corbett set up offices around the corner from the G&M building, on Trinity Street, in a modern office building owned by G&M. (The two buildings backed on to each other and were linked by a passageway.)

Field-Corbett and his company acted as company secretary to many of the companies which were making use of Traynor and his 'offshore' banking system. Many of these were also clients of Haughey Boland. As already mentioned, Furze would fly into Dublin a few times a year to go over the G&M books and reconcile them with the Cayman ones. Some evenings, Furze, Traynor, Field-Corbett and Collery and their respective wives would dine together. Field-Corbett also supplied services to the Haughey family, serving as a director of Larchfield Securities, a company used by the family to hold some of its assets, and of Abbeville Ltd, the company used to buy Haughey's Kinsealy estate. Over the years, Field-Corbett acted as a contact point for many customers who, by way of Traynor, had money stashed in the Cayman Islands.

The Ansbacher inspectors concluded that the schemes devised by Traynor facilitated the 'widespread evasion of tax' and that GMCT knowingly promoted tax evasion by its Irish clients. That said, it is very important to remember that not everyone who had dealings with Traynor or GMCT was necessarily involved in tax evasion. Though in broad terms the scheme was a tax evasion conspiracy, in each individual case that charge does not necessarily apply. This was stated by the inspectors at the end of their lengthy inquiry into Ansbacher, and is evident from the testimony given to the inspectors by some of the Ansbacher clients.

There was one further element to Traynor's operation. He began to open and close accounts in G&M in the name of companies called Amiens Securities and Amiens Investments. They were mostly Irish pound accounts and Traynor used them for 'switching' money between clients, without having to process currency exchanges or deal with the exchange control laws which existed. The Cayman accounts were, in the main, in sterling. If a client who had a Cayman account wanted to lodge IR£5,000, he could give it to Traynor who would put it in an Amiens account. If, some time later, a different client wanted IR£4,000, Traynor would give him the money from the Amiens account. The Amiens account would act as a sort of float. Meanwhile, the memorandum accounts and the accounts in the Cayman Islands would record the lodgement of the sterling equivalent of IR£5,000 to one Cayman account, and the withdrawal of the sterling equivalent of IR£4,000 from another Cayman account.

The Amiens accounts were also sometimes used as a sort of bridging point between clients and the Ansbacher Deposits. The Moriarty Tribunal heard numerous descriptions of money coming from Haughey's Ansbacher accounts by way of the Amiens accounts. The money would be transferred from the Ansbacher account to an Amiens account, and go from there to Haughey. A number of transactions might go through the same Amiens account with different people's money getting mixed at different times. In this way the link between the client and the Ansbacher Deposits was blurred.

People who wanted to make a withdrawal from their 'Cayman' accounts could ring Traynor or Williams and arrange a time and date for collecting their money. Sometimes large amounts of money were collected in cash. The cash was ordered by G&M from the Central

Bank and would be kept in the lobby for collection. Sometimes large amounts of cash, tens of thousands of pounds, were collected for Haughey in this manner. At other times people would collect drafts or, more commonly it seems, traveller's cheques. At other times again the money required would be transferred to an account in another bank, often in London.

For very large withdrawals, however, there was a danger that the attention of the Revenue would be drawn to what was a clandestine conspiracy aimed at keeping the existence of these dealings from the Revenue's attention. If, for instance, an individual or group of individuals or a company was to develop a site in Dublin using cash on deposit with GMCT, the Revenue might note the use of the cash during a review of the project, and begin to ask questions. This could lead not only to the discovery of the particular individual's offshore stash, but also to the existence of Traynor's secret onshore/offshore banking operation. To Traynor, however, this was just another difficulty which could be avoided with a bit of trickery while, at the same time, allowing for a further reduction in the amount of tax his clients would have to pay.

The system was simple. If someone had £2 million with GMCT, but needed £1 million of this to invest in some deal they were putting together, Traynor would organise a loan for that amount from G&M. The loan would be backed by a personal guarantee from the person receiving it and, perhaps, the asset being bought with the money. However, it would also, secretly, be backed by £1 million from the customer's Cayman account. That money would be transferred to Dublin and held until the loan was discharged. This cash backing for a loan of a similar amount would not be recorded on the bank's books. Instead a code was used in the memos drafted by the credit committee which oversaw and monitored the bank's loans. 'Suitably secured', or a variation of these words, conveyed to the members of the committee that the loan was backed by offshore cash linked, or hypothecated, to the loan. The bank made a small profit out of the arrangement, that being the difference between the amount of interest paid on the deposit and the amount of interest charged for the loan. The customer, on the other hand, if he, she or it wanted, could accumulate interest on the deposit and not pay tax on it, while charging the interest accumulated on the loan against tax. It was a neat trick, sneaking an extra tax benefit out of a tax scam. Within a few years of the scheme being put in place it was rumbled – but not by the Revenue.

3

Slipping the Net

A primary duty of the Central Bank was to ensure the stability of the State's banking system. In this role it would hold occasional on-site inspections of banks to establish the accuracy of their books and their overall stability. A key issue in this regard was the level of risk involved in a bank's loan book. In 1976 a number of Central Bank officials conducted an on-site inspection of G&M, and, while doing so, conducted an examination of the bank's loan book. The inspectors discovered a number of loans, some of them substantial, which were backed by offshore deposits. They became concerned that the bank was involved in an improper tax scheme.

Three chartered accountants took part in the inspection. They were Adrian Byrne, John Rockett and Bernard Daly. Byrne, currently the Head of Banking Supervision at the Central Bank, was the lead examiner. In the course of their detailed examination of the security which lay behind the loans on the G&M loan book, the Central Bank officials discovered the back-to-back nature of some of them. At the time, GMCT had £14.3 million on deposit with the Dublin bank, the examiners noted. The Ansbacher inspectors wrote: 'The clear impression gained by the bank examiners in relation to these deposits is that they were part of a scheme which was surrounded by a unique level of secrecy and which appeared to involve tax evasion.'

In their report the examiners wrote: 'We are satisfied from our conversations with Mr J D Traynor that a major part of these (G&M

s' activities is in the receipt of funds on which
avoided. The largest of the offshore subsidiaries is
ds company which we understand has received no
cheduled Territories since 22 June 1972 – the date
the Cay... ands became, in effect, a foreign state for exchange
control purposes... The bank is, in effect, offering a special service
which assists persons to transfer funds, on which tax has been
avoided, to offshore tax havens. The possibility of the bank abusing
its position as an authorised dealer in providing this service cannot
be ignored. In view of the delicate nature of these matters we did not
pursue the matter further.

'The directors of the bank were initially reluctant to give information about the activities of these companies to the Central Bank
because it feared that the information might be conveyed to the
revenue authorities. With regard to cases where loans by Guinness
& Mahon were secured by complex back-to-back arrangements of
deposits in these companies, we were given sight of copy security
documents but were requested not to note the names in which the
deposits were held. This we agreed to do. No files or records relating
to customer transactions with these companies are retained in
Dublin. The bank fears that the retention of such files would give
grounds to the Revenue to claim that the companies are managed by
Dublin and also individual files might come into the hands of the
revenue authorities...'

'We have been assured by Mr Traynor that no funds from Ireland
have been transferred to the Cayman Islands since 22 June 1972.

'Deposits held by the Cayman company have, however, increased
by £4.7 million to £14.3 million during the 12-month period to 31
March 1976. We have been assured that this increase has been
obtained through deposits from the United States and Jamaica. We
have no evidence to support this information.'

Byrne, who wrote the report, told the Ansbacher inspectors that
what the examiners found in G&M 'just didn't smell right... it didn't
taste right. There was something wrong.' He said the senior people
in the Central Bank to which the report was submitted were being

told, by way of the reference to the possibility that G&M was abusing its position as an authorised dealer, that G&M was possibly involved in tax evasion. Byrne told the inspectors that he had never before then, or since then, encountered such a concern among bankers for secrecy, or about the possibility that information might come into the hands of the Revenue.

The Governor of the Central Bank, Charles Murray, wrote to G&M expressing concern about its offshore activities. John Guinness wrote back, stating that he would 'not altogether be happy with your understanding of our situation in this regard and would certainly welcome an opportunity of discussing the matter.'

Eventually a meeting was held between senior figures from the Central Bank and G&M. A memo was written up afterwards by the Central Bank: 'Tax Havens. Mr Traynor outlined in some detail the operation of the bank's subsidiary companies in the Cayman Islands, Guernsey and Jersey. He stressed that they were basically trust companies but that a proportion of the assets being managed were deposited with the trust companies themselves. The three companies in question had banking status. He also emphasised that the funds were not placed on deposit for the purpose of tax avoidance or evasion. (Mr O'Grady-Walshe (the assistant director general) and I discussed this matter subsequently and agreed that we should talk with G&M again concerning this matter at a later date.)'

In January 1978 there was a meeting between Des Traynor and Maurice O'Kelly of G&M, and Timothy O'Grady-Walshe and Bernard Daly (manager of banking supervision) of the Central Bank, to discuss aspects of G&M's financial stability. (Maurice O'Kelly was a former Haughey Boland accountant who had been brought into G&M as an executive director by Traynor. He had left Haughey Boland some years before taking on the banking job.) During the meeting Traynor said G&M had approximately £4 million out in loans which were backed by Cayman cash deposits, and he argued that these loans should be considered risk-free. Mr Byrne wrote a report afterwards which included the following recommendation: 'From the information available, it would appear that the loans were secured by cash deposit and as such form a normal back-to-back arrangement. However, the fact that the bank takes such extreme precautions to keep the existence of the deposits secret from the Revenue Commissioners indicates that the bank might well be a party to a tax evasion scheme. Should this be the case and the bank accepts the right of set-off for the purposes of calculating the free resources ratio, the Bank would be placed in a very embarrassing position should the revenue authorities ever become aware of the situation. It is therefore recommended that the Bank does not accept a right of set-off for the purposes of calculating the free resources ratio.'

The free resources ratio is a banking measurement concerning the amount of capital a bank requires. When Byrne's report was filed, an official in the Central Bank crossed out the word evasion (an illegality) and inserted the word avoidance (which is not illegal). In Byrne's 1976 report a similar change had been made after he referred to possible tax evasion by way of G&M's Channel Island operations. Traynor was told by the Central Bank that the offshore deposit-backed G&M loans would continue to be regarded as carrying a risk.

Another on-site examination of the bank took place in June and July 1978 which again led to expressions of concern about the back-to-back loans. The final report said that the bank was involved in a tax avoidance scheme.

'We are of the view that while the provision of advice on tax avoidance within the law may be an acceptable part of the work of any bank, it is not, in our view, appropriate or ethical for a bank to participate in, as distinct from advise on, tax avoidance schemes. We suggest, therefore, that the bank should cease its participation in these schemes.' Byrne, who by this time had been promoted, was the official who reviewed the report. He told the Ansbacher inspectors that what this section of the report really meant was that G&M had crossed the line into tax evasion schemes.

During the 1978 inspection, G&M produced for the Central Bank officials a list of loans which were backed by offshore trust companies. The list included a loan of £416,000 to Ken O'Reilly-Hyland, which was backed by a Cayman deposit of £230,000. O'Reilly-Hyland, a successful businessman who had been a member of the Fianna Fáil fund-raising group, Taca, and had been involved in property developments along with Traynor and a number of others, was, at the time, a director of the Central Bank. The fact that one of its directors was involved in this scheme about which the Central Bank had such concerns, was recorded in the final report but not otherwise commented on. It led to no further internal correspondence within the Central Bank. The Ansbacher inspectors decided that the disclosure of this information to the Central Bank did not influence its view of G&M's activities.

O'Reilly-Hyland was not told by the Central Bank that it was aware of his dealings with G&M. He later told the Moriarty Tribunal and the Ansbacher inspectors that the trust in the Cayman Islands was established with after-tax money at around the time he became a Lloyds 'name'. Becoming a Lloyds name opened him to bankruptcy if his assets were ever called upon. He said that he informed the then Minister for Finance, George Colley, of the existence of the trust at the time he was appointed to the board of the Central Bank.

A further meeting between Traynor and O'Kelly and representatives of the Central Bank took place following the 1978 inspection. The Central Bank officials said it might request that G&M wind down its tax avoidance schemes. 'Mr Traynor said that such a request would make him very unhappy,' according to a Central Bank memo. 'He added that it was not correct to say that the bank was involved in any tax avoidance scheme.' The Central Bank subsequently wrote to John Guinness telling him it was unhappy with what was going on. 'We are of the view that there can be no reason for these arrangements other than to reduce the tax liabilities of the customers in question. It appears to the Central Bank that your bank's involvement in such arrangements is inappropriate and could be considered to be contrary to the national interest.'

A meeting took place between the two sides in March 1979. Traynor again argued that the loans were genuine banking loans. Both sides held their positions and an impasse seemed to be developing. Then Traynor said the level of loans which had cash deposits in offshore banks as security would not increase. He said no new loans backed by Cayman money had been issued since 1972, when the islands ceased being part of the sterling scheduled territories, and that the introduction of the new exchange control regulations (because of the Republic's break with sterling in 1978) would effectively end further loans being advanced where deposits held in the Channel Islands formed part of the security. On this basis, which implied that the level of such loans would decrease in the future, the Central Bank decided to let the matter rest.

Money belonging to Irish customers was, in fact, still being transferred to the Cayman Islands. Guinness Mahon Guernsey Ltd acted as trustee to hundreds of Channel Island discretionary trusts which in turn owned companies registered in the Cayman Islands. Money placed with the Channel Islands trusts might be placed with the Cayman companies, which would then put the money on deposit with G&M. In other words, despite what Traynor was telling the officials about exchange control and sterling areas, Irish customers' money was still being sent to the Cayman Islands.

Traynor was lying to the Central Bank officials. Not only was money still going to the Cayman Islands, new loans backed by Cayman deposits were being issued by G&M. He lied to the officials again during the 1982 inspection, when he again told them that no money had been transferred from Ireland to the Cayman Islands since 1972. At a meeting after the inspection, he told the Central Bank officials that there had been no increase in the type of lending which was causing concern. This was not correct. In fact, what had happened was that the bank was burying the fact of the backing for the loans even deeper than before.

By the mid-1980s the offshore subsidiaries were providing about half the profits being made by G&M. In 1984 the Central Bank was concerned about a number of bad debts which were emerging in the Dublin bank and threatening its stability. G&M was told that the Central Bank might want to extend its prudential supervision to GMCT. Before this matter developed, however, the Dublin bank sold its subsidiaries to its London parent, Guinness Mahon Co Ltd, for £4.7 million. One of the effects of this was that the supervision of GMCT now became a matter for the London regulatory authorities.

An inspection of G&M was conducted in 1986. The report recorded the sale of the Cayman subsidiary, the resignation of Maurice O'Kelly in the wake of the collapse of a textile company which had borrowings from the bank, and the announcement that Traynor was resigning as chief executive and deputy chairman of G&M. A misleading list of back-to-back loans was furnished to the Central Bank. This happened again during an inspection in February 1988.

The Central Bank always had open to it the option of asking for the resignations of directors it felt were not suitable people to be involved in the banking industry. However, a difficulty with this was that such a move could spark the collapse of a bank, and trying to prevent such occurrences was at the heart of the work of the Central Bank. It was not open to the Central Bank to notify the Revenue of its suspicions in relation to the loans it had examined in G&M – a point Traynor had made sure to emphasise to the Central Bank officials who conducted the 1970s examinations. At the time the Revenue would not have been allowed to conduct a general examination of the G&M operation. The law only allowed the Revenue to examine the affairs of an individual or company from which it wished to collect taxes. Even to examine a particular person's bank files, the Revenue first had to get an order from the High Court. The law has since been changed, largely due to the discovery of the Ansbacher Deposits, and the Revenue can now, with the permission of the High Court, examine a class of accounts, such as the loans issued by G&M, if it can show that it has grounds for suspicion.

The misleading details given by G&M to the Central Bank concerning its back-to-back loans did, in fact, illustrate that, while the overall amount of such loans might not be increasing, there were new loans being issued after Traynor had promised this would not occur. A further point of note is that an internal Guinness Mahon London audit, which included a review of the Dublin bank, described in detail the secret memorandum account operation run by Traynor and Pádraig Collery, and expressed concerns about it. In essence, what the internal audit report discovered was that the Cayman bank was operating in the Republic without a banking licence, an offence under the Central Bank Acts. There is no evidence that the Central Bank ever sought or received a copy of the audit report. If it had, then what its reaction would have been is a matter of speculation. At the time, 1989, Mr Haughey, by then an Ansbacher account holder, was Taoiseach.

The Central Bank told the Ansbacher inspectors what, in hindsight, would have happened if all that G&M was up to had been discovered at the time. It said it would have 'conducted a thorough investigation of G&M with a view to ensuring that persons concerned in the unlawful activities and the deception practised on the Central Bank would have no place in the banking industry, and to take any necessary legal proceedings and also to cooperate with the Director of Public Prosecutions in any criminal investigation.'

The inspectors, in their review of the Central Bank's performance in relation to the matter, said it was commendable that the Central Bank had noted the backed loans and had developed the correct suspicions. Traynor had protested that the arrangements were innocent, but the Central Bank had not believed him. It had, however, accepted his subsequent assurance that the volume of the loans would not be allowed to increase and would decrease over time. 'It was unwise of, and regrettable for the Central Bank to have accepted Mr Traynor's representations, particularly in circumstances where the bank already harboured reservations about his protestations of innocence regarding the back-to-back deposits.'

False information concerning the backed loans was, over the coming years, supplied to the Central Bank by G&M, but even this information, if analysed, would have demonstrated that Traynor's representations were inaccurate. The inspectors' overall conclusion in relation to the Central Bank's performance was: 'A combination of the misleading information furnished by G&M and in particular Mr Traynor and a failure on the part of the Central Bank to test, appraise and gather the information available to it resulted in the true nature of Ansbacher's activities going undetected for longer than ought to have been the case.'

The Central Bank was the only authority which ever came close to discovering what Des Traynor was up to. Even now we don't know the full picture. However, thanks to the Ansbacher inspectors' report, we do have testimony from quite a few of Traynor's customers as to what it was like to do business with him and G&M in the 1970s, 1980s and 1990s. It is a fascinating insight into an aspect of Irish life in certain circles during a particular period. The picture which emerges is grotesque, bizarre and often beggars belief. When considering the picture, it is useful to bear in mind the political context within which all this occurred.

4

Politics and Money

In the early 1930s a political donation of what was then a very large amount of money, £500, was sent by cheque to Fianna Fáil headquarters by Joe McGrath, the operator of the very successful Hospital Sweepstakes. McGrath, who was a Cumann na nGaedheal supporter, sent the cheque without notifying anyone of his intention. The party general secretary was a bit concerned when he received the cheque, because of the size of the donation, and he raised the matter with Gerry Boland, father of Kevin Boland. Kevin Boland recounted the incident in his book, *The Rise and Decline of Fianna Fáil* (Mercier Press, 1982). Gerry Boland was one of the party's general secretaries and when he was shown the cheque and asked what to do with it his reply was immediate: 'Send it back'. The money was returned by post, with a polite note explaining that it was not party policy to accept such large donations.

The other joint general secretary of the party at the time was Seán Lemass. He raised the issue at the subsequent meeting of the party's national executive and after the meeting it was decided that the donation should be accepted. McGrath was asked to send the cheque again, which he did.

Kevin Boland wrote that it was from this point on that his father noticed a gradual change in character in Fianna Fáil. He said that McGrath, with whom Lemass was friendly despite the men having fought on opposite sides in the Civil War, had no unworthy motive in sending the large donation. One of the reasons McGrath was liked by former Republicans was because he made use of a lot of Republicans who had fled the state after the war to sell Sweepstakes tickets in the US and Canada. The use of the men was an astute move and was a significant contributor to the commercial success of the Sweepstakes, while at the same time it provided a good standard of living for many of the exiled combatants.

Boland pointed out in his book that Fine Gael always had the support of wealthy donors. As the economic policies of Fianna Fáil changed and brought about improvements – largely under the leader-ship of Lemass – the ranks of the upper classes were 'infiltrated' by newcomers who had not inherited their wealth, but had rather become well-off by way of the mix of their own enterprise and government policy. Many of these people, naturally, became sub-scribers to Fianna Fáil's fund-raising efforts.

In time, an election finance committee was formed, an ad hoc group of business people who collected money from their colleagues around election times. Then, later, a group was formed in Dublin called Comh-Comhairle Átha Cliath. The subscription fee was con-siderable, £10 per annum, and the members were often not signed-up members of Fianna Fáil. In return for their support, these people got access to government ministers and were invited to attend lectures and discussions. Some party members objected to the new group, feeling that it represented a downgrading of the ordinary party member. The first meeting of the new group heard a speech from Lemass where he argued that with the correct investment of their money, the business classes could create 100,000 new jobs.

What happened next was to become the cause of great scandal. There was a referendum on changing the voting system, after which the Fianna Fáil coffers were less than full. The party's national execu-tive considered the issue, and in 1966 decided to study the idea of the Comh-Comhairle Átha Cliath group or commission being given some sort of formal footing and being established on a permanent basis. In time, it was decided to invite 500 business figures to join a new Fianna Fáil fund-raising group and that each member would have to pay an annual subscription of £100. The group was to be called Taca, meaning help, or support, in Irish.

The group was formed without any publicity. It was decided that it would hold occasional lunches or dinners in Dublin city-centre hotels. These occasions were not advertised and were supposed to take place out of the public gaze. However, the press got wind of what was going on and the story grew wings. The opposition dubbed the Taca membership, many of whom were property developers and builders, the 'tacateers' and there were cries of corruption and talk of £100-a-plate dinners. Boland was one of the signatories of the group's bank accounts. The others were Jack Lynch and Neil Blaney. Blaney and Charles Haughey were patrons of the group and Kevin Boland's brother, Harry Boland, was secretary and treasurer. The opening dinner was attended by the entire government.

According to Boland, the creation of Taca was more about the changing nature of the party than about corruption. The people who joined the group were already supporters of the party and were already making donations. The significance of the development was that it marked the maturation of the patronising of the party by business leaders. In time, he wrote, the party became dependent on the services which it bought with the money subscribed and, thereby, became dependent on the people who were making the donations. It is, of course, a development which occurred in most western democracies during the course of the Twentieth century and is one which has many critics, arguably with very good reason.

The 1960s was a time of great change in the Republic. Miniskirts, youth culture and the initial challenges to authority all arrived in Ireland. So too did money, or the ability to make profits. A number of people who began to make significant amounts of money associated with Fianna Fáil because they saw themselves as part of a political programme, and because they thought being close to the party was in their interest.

The chairman of the secret committee which ran Taca was Desmond MacGreevy, of MacGreevy and Partners, a firm of quantity surveyors and construction economists. Among the members of the committee were: Ken O'Reilly-Hyland; Noel Griffin of Waterford Glass; Sam Stephenson, architect; John Reihill, of Tedcastle, McCormack and Co Ltd; Liam McGonagle, solicitor; Dillon Digby of First National Building Society; Eoin Kenny of J A Kenny and Partners; and Denis McCarthy, of Odearest. Of these, O'Reilly-Hyland, Stephenson, McGonagle and McCarthy were all to be later named as clients of Traynor and Ansbacher Cayman.

A lot of the business figures who were associated with Taca and Fianna Fáil would socialise in Dublin in the Russell Hotel, on St Stephen's Green (since demolished), the Gresham Hotel on O'Connell Street, and Groome's Hotel, on Cavendish Row, now Cassidy's Hotel. Fianna Fáil ministers, deputies and senators, as well as a number of these business figures, would often meet for after-hours drinking in Groome's, which was owned by a long-time party supporter. Gardai who had the misfortune to poke their noses in would put themselves in danger of a transfer to Connacht.

Patrick Gallagher, the son of the property developer and builder, Matt Gallagher, gave an insightful interview about this period to the *Sunday Business Post* in the late 1990s. The interview was conducted by the journalist Frank Connolly, over drinks in a hotel in Zimbabwe, where Gallagher was living at the time. Gallagher explained that his father, Matt Gallagher, was a friend and supporter of Fianna Fáil who had returned from England to take part in the economic renaissance Lemass wished to bring about. He'd become very rich in the process. He devoted one day out of every month to Taca business.

According to Patrick Gallagher, the group his father belonged to saw themselves as part of a movement to create a more prosperous Ireland. In the 1950s the southern Irish economy was in a terrible state, with ships leaving Irish ports every week carrying live cattle and emigrating citizens. The State's coffers were dependent on the excise raised from alcohol and tobacco sales. The men who were gathered around Lemass, Fianna Fáil and Taca wished to transform the situation, while in the process becoming rich and creating a new ownership or capitalist class which was nationalist and Catholic in background. As part of this programme, Haughey was to be sponsored in his climb up the political ladder and his career in politics generally. Haughey, from this perspective, was one of the group, and unique in that he was going to leave business to go full-time into politics. The deal was, according to this version of events, that Haughey would be looked after so that, despite his choice, he would continue to live the expensive lifestyle the others within the group expected and were able to pay for themselves.

'Haughey was financed in order to create the environment which the Anglo-Irish had enjoyed and that we as a people could never aspire to,' Gallagher told Connolly. The new Ireland and the new more prosperous Irish would take the place of the Anglo-Irish, moving into their mansions and their country estates. Gallagher described the renovation by the State of the Royal Hospital, Kilmainham, Government Buildings and Dublin Castle as being part of, or belonging to, this broad programme.

'Everything was planned. Somebody had to live in the big house and Haughey created a marvellous situation with these projects at Kilmainham, Dublin Castle and the Taoiseach's [office]. Our contribution was the RHA.' The RHA Gallagher Gallery, on Ely Place in Dublin, was funded by the Gallagher group.

Ironically, many of the business figures associated with the group, and who had made fortunes which allowed them live in large Georgian mansions, made part of their money by knocking down parts of Georgian Dublin to make room for office developments. At the time, although it was opposed by others, this was seen by some as a positive development, since the new office buildings were associated with the new State and the old buildings were associated with the years of English oppression.

According to Gallagher, it was part of the plan that Des Traynor would look after Haughey's personal finances while Haughey looked after affairs of state. During the 1960s Traynor became a director of, and small shareholder in, the Gallagher group and was devoting one day a week, at least, to its affairs. Traynor provided tax advice to both the group and to Matt and, subsequently, Patrick Gallagher. He joined the company as a director in 1961, at a time when he was a partner in Haughey Boland and was living in a house built by the Gallaghers at 12 Raheny Park.

In 1959, while he was still an active partner with his accountancy firm, Haughey bought a house near Raheny, in north Dublin, called Grangemore. The house was large and stood on 45 acres of land. According to Patrick Gallagher, it was his father who told Haughey to buy the property, telling him that in time the group would buy it back from him for a substantially increased sum. This indeed is what happened. Haughey bought the property for £10,000, a large amount of money when a TD's salary at the time amounted to less than £1,500 per annum. In time, the land was re-zoned, with permission given for the construction of up to 386 houses. Haughey sold Grangemore in 1969, ten years after buying it, for £204,000. The Gallagher group bought it via Merchant Banking, the bank on which Traynor sat as a director. Haughey was Minister for Finance at the time, and during the run-up to the 1969 general election the Fine Gael director of elections, Gerald Sweetman, made much of the sale. He claimed Haughey had avoided paying tax on his windfall as a result of a measure introduced by him in the 1968 Finance Act. Haughey issued a 'categorical denial' that he had used his position for his own benefit. Lynch defended his minister in the Dáil, saying Haughey was 'a well-off man before he became a minister in our government, and he would be a far better-off man if he never took office in government.'

A year before the sale of Grangemore, Haughey bought a 127-acre stud farm in Ratoath, Co. Meath, without taking out a mortgage. The farm cost £30,000, at a time when Haughey's salary as a minister was £3,500 and he was no longer making an income from Haughey Boland. Charles Haughey made a lot of money in the 1960s. The Moriarty Tribunal, which was charged with investigating Haughey's personal finances, was only charged with examining the period 1979 to 1996. The truth about Haughey and money in the 1960s will probably never be known.

One of the opponents of Taca within the Fianna Fáil party was George Colley, the man who would become a rival to Haughey for the leadership of the party. Colley suspected that Haughey was making money by facilitating State leases on office blocks built or planned by his business friends. With just an option to buy a site, a company could make a significant profit if it could secure a commitment to a 35-year lease from the State on a building planned for the site. This was the equivalent to the kind of bonanza which can result from a change in the zoning of land. At one stage, Colley ruled that all commitments to leases on buildings by the State had to be passed across his desk because of concerns he had about Haughey.

Some in the party believed that Taca was causing them damage electorally, and there were calls for its abolition. In December 1968, following a Fianna Fáil parliamentary party discussion on the issue, the party leader, Jack Lynch, announced some changes to the group that would make it more attractive to the general party membership. He also hit out at the organisation's critics. It was an essential part of democracy that people should be able to voluntarily support the party which appeared to them to have the best policies for the development of the country, he said. 'It is a shameful thing that these people have been so irresponsibly and unscrupulously attacked in an organised campaign of personal detraction that has never been paralleled in this country... I want to say categorically that no member of Taca has benefited in any way from his membership, nor do I believe any member ever expected to so benefit.'

When, at an Árd Fheis in the late 1960s, delegates criticised Taca, saying that the party was forgetting the ordinary man for whom it had been established, Neil Blaney replied that the people who made up Taca were ordinary people who had prospered because of the policies of Fianna Fáil. It was right that they should want to give something back to the party that had made their success possible, he said.

In 1969, Jack Lynch asked the Fianna Fáil senator and businessman, Des Hanafin, to take over as paid secretary of Taca. Hanafin agreed. He was a successful hotelier who had spotted an opportunity to make some money leasing heavy machinery, and had done so. He was also recovering from a battle with alcoholism, a fight he would win. The first thing Hanafin did was change the name of the Fianna Fáil group he was now in charge of. He felt the name Taca played into the hands of political opponents of Fianna Fáil. The new group was called the Fianna Fáil General Election Fund-Raising Committee. He cancelled the secret dinners which had been such a godsend to press and opposition alike. Functions held by the newly-named group were publicly announced and the press took little interest in them. Otherwise, little changed. Most of the same supporters continued to support Fianna Fáil. O'Reilly-Hyland, McGonagle, Reihill and McCarthy continued to work on the committee. Other members included Gerry Creedon, of Gypsum Industries, Roy Donovan of Lisney and Sons and a governor of the Central Bank, and Beamish & Crawford chairman, Clayton Love. Working from room 547 in the Burlington Hotel – part of the Doyle group – the collection of money from business figures continued as before.

According to Kevin Boland, it was when the 1973-1977 Fine Gael/Labour coalition government, and the then Finance Minister, Richie Ryan, in particular, introduced new taxes on wealth and capital gains, that the money really began to flow into Fianna Fáil's coffers. The changes introduced by the coalition's taxation policies led to a panic-stricken, headlong rush towards Fianna Fáil. These were people, according to Boland, whose only interest was their own interests and who saw themselves as making an investment from which they expected a return. Hanafin, who was overseeing the taking-in of the money, does not agree with this. His view is that the people who donated money to the party never sought anything in return.

In December 1979 Haughey won the leadership of Fianna Fáil in a battle with George Colley. The vote was close. The Moriarty Tribunal later revealed that Haughey had run up a huge overdraft with AIB during the 1970s, and only turned his mind to settling the debt when the leadership battle was about to begin. His bank manager, Michael Phelan, kept a diary around this period and noted some of his dealings or conversations with Haughey. In late September 1979 he noted in relation to Haughey: 'Borrowing abroad – G Colley.' What this meant is not clear. He also noted conversations where Haughey assured him that Patrick Gallagher was going to come up with some money, and that Traynor was on the case. When Haughey won the leadership, Gallagher made a payment of £300,000, in what some people thought was a bogus land deal. Whatever the truth of that, the Gallagher group never got anything in return for the money and Haughey got to keep it. A bank account to receive money from donors to help Haughey clear his overdraft with AIB, was opened on the same day that Haughey was elected Taoiseach for the first time. £780,662 was lodged to the G&M account, which was managed by Traynor. After AIB had been paid off, Haughey was left with £30,662 to spend on himself.

Once in the leadership position, Haughey set about getting control of the party's fund-raising activities and finances. He had played a significant role in Taca, but had been out in the cold following the Arms Crisis in 1970. Now that he was leader of the party he wanted to know who was contributing to the party, and take control of the fund-raising effort. Hanafin resisted, and Colley, Haughey's opponent in the tight leadership struggle, was also opposed to the move. There was a book, known as the Black Book, which contained details of the various subscribers to the party. A 15-month battle ensued before Haughey wrested it from Hanafin's hands. Before the full information fell into Haughey's hands, however, it is believed that Haughey gained access to a list of the subscribers, but not the details of how much they donated. How he managed this has never been discovered.

In February 1982, following a general election and an abortive leadership challenge by Des O'Malley, Haughey told Hanafin that he was fired as secretary of the fund-raising committee. Hanafin was an O'Malley supporter. Haughey also told Hanafin that the chairman of the committee, Ken O'Reilly-Hyland, was sacked and that he was going to disband the committee. However, Hanafin argued that the committee was independent of the party and the leadership, and that Haughey had no power to sack him.

A short time afterwards, Haughey invited O'Reilly-Hyland and the other members of the committee to his home in Kinsealy. He invited them down to the bar, which had been built in an old sewing room in the house. He asked the members who'd turned up to sign a document calling on Hanafin to hand over the complete fund-raising accounts to the Fianna Fáil HQ in Mount Street. One of those present, Gerry Creedon, of Gypsum Industries, refused. The others did as Haughey requested. Afterwards they went to have dinner in a private room in Johnny Oppermann's restaurant in Malahide. Hanafin, when he heard what had happened, refused to hand over the book until the accounts had been fully audited.

Creedon and Gerry Hickey (another Ansbacher client) resigned from the committee after the removal of Hanafin. Sam Stephenson, Dillon Digby and Eoin Kenny ceased to act on the committee soon afterwards. Haughey, it seems, wanted to make the whole operation bigger, with a manager, staff and new, larger fund-raising schemes, but this never materialised. In time he appointed his own fund-raiser, Paul Kavanagh, a businessman who owned a successful printing business, and who sought no payment for his work on the party's behalf. Hanafin found that once the battle between himself and Haughey was over, Haughey seemed to bear no grudge. Overall, Hanafin felt, Haughey was a man who wanted to do good for the country.

From the 1960s onwards, Traynor was involved in raising money for Haughey's personal use. Haughey told the tribunal that he trusted Traynor not to approach a political opponent when he was looking for money. 'Mr Traynor would certainly have been wise enough and experienced enough to know not to go to somebody who might be politically hostile to me.' Given the sensitivity and nature of what was involved, and the need for discretion, one class of person Traynor might have felt comfortable approaching would be the rich people whose financial affairs he handled, and especially those who had funds placed through him in the Ansbacher Deposits.

Traynor's closeness to Haughey may have been an aspect of what made it attractive to have him as a business associate and advisor. Giving money to Haughey, through Traynor, would make you a fully-paid-up member of the club.

Traynor, Haughey said, was not particularly interested in politics. 'He was always very insistent that he was not a political person and that in so far as he would make any sort of contribution to our country's affairs, it would be through relieving me of financial responsibilities and handling them himself. He felt that that was the best way he could contribute to his country's well being.'

The Ansbacher Deposits and the 'golden circle' around Haughey, that many believed existed, were not one and the same thing. A good number of the people who gave money to Traynor for lodgement offshore had nothing to do with Fianna Fáil or Haughey. However, the people who were named in the Ansbacher inspectors' report as having been customers of the Cayman bank's Irish operations included a number of people who were at the heart of the Haughey/Taca/Fianna Fáil fund-raising scene from the 1960s to the 1980s. There was common ground between Taca and Ansbacher, and between Ansbacher and the people who gave money to Haughey. Given the size of the economy at the time it would be surprising if it were otherwise. Nevertheless, the fact remains that such a group existed.

Part Two

Why Everyone Needs a Good Accountant

5

Members of the Club

The story of how the Fitzwilliam Lawn Tennis Club in south Dublin came to be where it is was outlined in Frank McDonald's book, *The Destruction of Dublin* (Gill & Macmillan, 1985). The story begins with Sir Basil Goulding, a baronet and pillar of the business community, who was chairman of Gouldings Fertilisers. In 1964, just a few weeks before a new planning act came into force, he secured permission for a thirteen-storey office development at Wilton Place, between Fitzwilliam Square and the Grand Canal. Houses which stood on the site were demolished and, despite the efforts of the writer, Mary Lavin, who lived nearby, a 75,000 square foot office block was built on the site. Goulding took up office in a suite on the top floor.

From his new offices, Goulding could see the Fitzwilliam Lawn Tennis Club below and muse about its development potential. He was the club's president, and in 1969 he put a proposal to its executive committee that the club give up its Wilton Place site and receive, in return, a new club-house and courts on a 2.5 acre site he owned on Burlington Road, across the canal. It would probably have been a profitable venture for Goulding, but within a few days a counter proposal was put to the committee which it was unable to refuse.

The new offer came from Ken O'Reilly-Hyland, chairman of Burmah Castrol (Ireland) Ltd, Fianna Fáil fund raiser, and also a member of the Fitzwilliam club. He was supported in his venture by

Fianna Fáil senator Eoin Ryan, who was chairman of New Ireland Assurance, of which Des Traynor was also a director, and the architects, Sam Stephenson and Arthur Gibney. All were members of the club.

In return for the club's site, this team were offering a 4.5 acre site bounded by Winton Road and Appian Way, a new clubhouse with all facilities, and £300,000 in cash. The bulk of the site offered was accounted for by the extensive rear gardens of four Victorian houses on Winton Road, three of which were the offices of Stephenson and Gibney, and the fourth of which was Ryan's home.

The deal was one of the factors behind the establishment of a company called Marlborough Holdings. The company was set up by the solicitor and friend of Charles Haughey's, Liam McGonagle, and its directors included, Ryan, for New Ireland Assurance, Des Traynor, then still a partner in Haughey Boland, and Ken O'Reilly-Hyland. The bulk of the company's shares were held in the name of the Guinness & Mahon company, Mars Nominees.

Ken O'Reilly-Hyland had been involved in a property development with McGonagle in Donnybrook earlier in the 1960s. He moved from a large house in Milltown, Dublin, to a stately home, Ounavarra, near Gorey, Co.Wexford, after getting planning permission for flats in the grounds of his former home. This was done, with his involvement being kept secret, through the offices of the estate agents, Finnegan Menton. O'Reilly-Hyland had made a lot of money. He was Master of the Fox Hounds of the Meath Hunt and a Knight of Malta. He was on the boards of the Central Bank and Aer Lingus. In Dublin, he lived in a mansion on Ailesbury Road. Ironically, according to Frank McDonald, some of the more ugly ventures O'Reilly-Hyland was involved in, received planning permission through the intervention of Kevin Boland, who disliked the 'earls' who complained about the destruction of Georgian Dublin.

Ken O'Reilly-Hyland and the auctioneer John Finnegan were involved in the building of Telephone House, an office block on Marlborough Street built by a company called Marlborough Estates (separate from Marlborough Holdings). The building was pre-let to the Department of Post and Telegraphs before construction work had started in 1969. This deal was organised by Finnegan, the force behind Finnegan Menton. O'Reilly-Hyland was also involved in a property near Harold's Cross Bridge, the former Greenmount oil company site, where in 1969 he tried to build a huge office, shops and residential accommodation complex. Planning permission was refused, however, and the site was passed on to a company called Echo Holdings, a £2 company, the directors of which were the solicitor, Pat O'Connor, and his son. O'Connor was a friend and neighbour of Haughey's who was later charged with double voting in the 1982 general election. In 1980, Finnegan Menton sold the property for £1.3 million. Before the sale, the O'Connors were replaced on the board of Echo Holdings by two accountants from Management Investment Services, the company run by former Haughey Boland employee, Sam Field-Corbett. In 1983, Pat O'Connor issued a statement prompted by media speculation: 'Neither Mr Haughey, any member of his family nor any person or body corporate on his behalf have at any time, directly or indirectly, had any interest in Echo Holdings Ltd or in the (Greenmount) property.'

The Ansbacher Report identified almost everyone mentioned above as having been clients of Ansbacher. The exceptions were Goulding, Ryan, Boland and the O'Connors. Profits from property deals the people named in the report were involved in were lodged through Traynor in Cayman Islands trusts. According to Gibney, Traynor was the central figure in the organisation of the financial aspects of these projects, borrowing money if borrowing was required, coordinating financial inputs and distributing profits. Traynor was central to bringing the group together.

Sam Stephenson told the inspectors that Traynor was a close partner and friend of his around this time, and was of great benefit as an advisor. The inspectors produced a G&M memo from May 1976 which showed that Stephenson, his partner, Gibney, and their firm between them had loans totalling £600,000 from the bank. They were, in part, backed by offshore trust funds totalling £332,376. Stephenson told the inspectors that he remembered Traynor telling him he should set up a trust, but couldn't remember if it had been set up or not. The £332,376, he said, he would have thought were his and Gibney's deposits in GMCT. He said that he was told early in the 1970s that he had £150,000 on deposit in Cayman.

'Mr Traynor was first of all our accountant and we became involved in a number of property transactions. We made profits on some, considerable profits on others, and subsequently I understand we lost it all in a number of ventures around about 1973 with the decline in the property market... Whatever arrangements were made in relation to the deposits in the Cayman Islands I understood it was perfectly legal and legitimate at the time that money which we made... the principal money that I remember we made was on the Fitzwilliam Lawn Tennis Club transaction, and I understand the figure that I made there together with the other six partners was about £100,000.'

He said that Traynor transferred his, Stephenson's, portion of the profits from the Fitzwilliam deal to the Cayman Islands and that Stephenson never asked advice from any other party in relation to the matter. He trusted Traynor. 'We were very close friends and I was very grateful for his advice... Mr Traynor would have transferred (the profits) on my behalf if they were transferred in that sense. I understood the Cayman Islands was a kind of lump of sand in the middle of the Pacific.'

When the Fitzwilliam deal had been put to bed the partners involved gathered to celebrate, and to be told by Traynor what their cut of the profits was. 'There was a dinner party and he was informing everybody of what their share of the profits would be and I think he scribbled it on a piece of paper. It had about £110,000 on it,' Stephenson said. His money was transferred to the Cayman Islands but he never got a statement of his account. 'The only occasion I remember him giving me a piece of paper with a figure on it was when we were celebrating the result of the Fitzwilliam deal.' As future amounts were added, smaller amounts from smaller deals, the balances were verbally conveyed to Stephenson.

'I understood when this was discussed that this was perfectly legal to deposit funds overseas, they would not be liable for tax, they could be used for back-to-back loans if we wished to do so, but that if they were repatriated to the country we would then be liable for tax on them. That is the position as I understood it. As explained to me, I think certainly Mr Traynor and I think the tax advisor at the time was a partner in Stokes Kennedy Crowley who set up this system, I think.' He said Don Reid was the partner, and he remembered being in a meeting with Reid and Traynor in the Stephenson and Gibney offices. 'He was the leading tax advisor in Dublin at the time... This was perfectly legal. It avoided tax but if it was repatriated to the country it would then incur tax.' Reid was not his accountant but was advising Traynor, Stephenson said. 'I understood that a number of people were receiving this advice in Dublin at the time.'

Stephenson's money was under Traynor's control. 'Our relationship was one of very close partnership and he was a great asset and of great benefit to us both as an accountant and as an advisor.' When matters were going well they would buy and sell sites and make profits without conducting any development. Traynor would sometimes meet Stephenson for breakfast at 7.00 am in Stephenson's mews home in Ballsbridge and the two men would discuss deals. Gibney said that Traynor was a sort of mentor to Stephenson. However, when the property market crashed in the mid-1970s, Stephenson found it hard to deal with.

'Some of these transactions went very well, and then they went sour in the property crash of 1974/1975, and my relationship with Mr Traynor soured very considerably when he told me one evening in my home [...] I actually agreed to sell a farm I had in Carlow, Ballynoe, to cover our losses [...] but when he actually told me in my home that my house would have to go, I was really stunned.'

'He had advised me some years earlier to leave the deeds of the Mews, which was my residence in Dublin, with Guinness & Mahon, (it had no borrowings at all), for security, because at that time it looked like I might be sued for very substantial sums of money, arising out of professional indemnity, possibly claims. However, when he told me that that property now was securing borrowings that we had made with Guinness & Mahon, I was pretty well upset and I just terminated at that stage and I threatened to sue him. I said, 'You can't take my home. You know that that was never intended to be a security for any of these loans, I am losing enough as it is, and I will certainly fight you tooth and nail if you try to use those deeds.' Eventually he either relented or recognised the situation but we parted on that basis.'

Stephenson got back his deeds and Traynor took everything else that the architect had on deposit in G&M/GMCT. The inspectors told Stephenson that it was possible that Traynor had established a trust for him in the Cayman Islands without telling him, as he had done this for other people also.

Arthur Gibney told the inspectors that he, too, had become involved with GMCT as a result of the property deals he was involved in. He said that Traynor had suggested that he form a family trust. Traynor was interested in setting up his own trust. 'He was particularly concerned, I think, because his health hadn't been very good. He had, I think, had a heart attack just when he had, [...] as he went into Guinness & Mahon he had a very serious coronary condition.' He said that at the time he was told about the trust idea by Traynor and by Don Reid, and that G&M were setting up an office in the Cayman Islands at the time. He wasn't sure if a trust was ever set up but money was sent out to Cayman. In fact, a trust *was* established. Money was sent out from the profits of the sale of the three houses and gardens used in the Fitzwilliam deal.

The consortium did not develop the original site of the Fitzwilliam Lawn Tennis Club, but sold it on. Similarly, other deals did not involve development, but profits were made from the buying and selling-on of the sites. The only deal that actually resulted in a completed development was the construction of an office block on Bride Street. The office block was sold on to New Ireland Assurance, of which Traynor was a director, and Stephenson and Gibney shared the profits.

Later, in the mid-1970s, when the property market collapsed, Gibney's offshore deposits were eaten up by trying to satisfy his bank debts. Traynor told Gibney that he appreciated his co-operation in relation to trying to settle the debts and was going to set aside £25,000 for him. 'When I found myself in this situation I had also found that myself and Mr Stephenson weren't getting on in terms of what we both wanted to do... We fell out and we decided we were, I was going to leave the partnership. One of the problems that accrued was when Guinness & Mahon looked for their money back – I think Guinness & Mahon were probably in difficulties. They had been involved in a lot of property development other than the ones they were involved in with us. I think there were difficulties there because I think two of their senior people had to leave.'

'I think Desmond Traynor was retained because he was probably not terribly involved. He was more involved in the financial end of it rather than the sort of property development end. At this stage, Mr Stephenson really felt we were not being treated properly by Guinness & Mahon. He disputed figures and disputed the fact that he owed this money. I wanted to get shut of the whole thing... One of the problems I encountered was that in the settlement, after I sold property in Wexford, sold property in Clontarf, was that my home, which was a mews in Leeson Place, was also in question. Mr Traynor demanded that – they had the deeds of all my properties but he wanted the deeds of my home... it ended up with my mews being mortgaged to pay the debts to Citibank. At this stage I was more or less bankrupt.'

Arthur Gibney was trying to start up a new practice, and his solicitor, Terence Doyle, who was also solicitor to Gibney's wife, went to see Traynor. Doyle argued that Gibney was in a particularly difficult position because he and Stephenson had fallen out, and Stephenson was resisting throwing everything into the pot to clear the debts, while Gibney was going along with Traynor's demands. 'And Mr Traynor said: "Yes. I agree. Mr Gibney has been very cooperative. He has done his best to pay off the stuff. I agree his mews is in danger".' Traynor called in Gibney and told him he was going to set aside £25,000 just in case Gibney lost his mews. Asked where the money was being set aside from, Gibney said he wasn't too clear. 'I mean I was so glad to be reassured at the time. Mr Traynor to a great extent doesn't [...] didn't explain a lot of the things he did.'

Gibney set about establishing his new practice. As far as he was concerned, the £25,000 put aside was not his but might come into play if he got into trouble with his mews repayments. Stephenson, meanwhile, was repaying money he owed to Citibank arising out of the same property developments. When he had completed that process it seems that the £25,000 became available to Gibney. The architect had not seen Traynor much after the 1970s property market collapse, but in the early 1980s he got a call from Traynor who asked if Gibney would do some work on his house. Stephenson and Gibney had done a huge extension to the large house on the Howth Road which Traynor had bought in 1970. Now there were problems, and Traynor asked Gibney to sort them out. 'I went to his house,' Gibney said, 'and he told me then: "By the way, that money is there. It is in your name".' Traynor was referring to the £25,000, which was now in an account in the Ansbacher Deposits.

Gibney once went to Traynor and suggested that he withdraw all the money. 'I said can I invest some of that money in a pension fund and he said, look, listen, he said, pensions you are throwing your money away, particularly at your age, he said. You can have the money, he said, as part of a pension fund when you retire.'

Gibney said that Traynor wasn't an intimidating person. 'I think he was a very ordinary person but in my terms, he intimidated me about money and my lack of knowledge of the financial world. I looked upon him as a great benefactor at the time because he had been extremely generous to me. He had helped me at a time when I was virtually bankrupt and I treated him with great respect... He had a reputation as a whizz-kid.'

Ken O'Reilly-Hyland told the inspectors that he established a trust in the Bahamas in the 1960s, because he became a Lloyds name in 1963. Being a name means that you can benefit from profits from the Lloyds insurance business but have an unlimited liability if the Lloyds business your group is linked to makes a loss. As the entire assets of Lloyds names can be called upon if the insurance firm finds itself in difficulty, O'Reilly-Hyland created his trust, he said, so as to prevent his being made a bankrupt in the event of Lloyds hitting the rocks. He put £100,000 sterling into the trust in 1964. The beneficiaries were to be his family, and the trust was run by a firm of attorneys in Nassau. In early 1966, O'Reilly-Hyland mentioned to John Guinness that he had a trust in the Bahamas and Guinness said in response that his bank had it in mind to establish an offshore trust management service. Guinness said he had an excellent investment team and that O'Reilly-Hyland might at some stage think about transferring his fund to them. This happened in the early 1970s, partly because O'Reilly-Hyland was unhappy with how his Nassau trust was being managed. The new trust was set up with GMCT, and a shelf company, Newport Agencies (Overseas) Ltd, was assigned to the trust.

O'Reilly-Hyland said that he first met Traynor during the 1960s, when Traynor was working with Haughey Boland. 'It was politic to give some work to Haughey Boland, which I did, and I met him in a very perfunctory way. It was a very small account. They were not my personal accountants.'

O'Reilly-Hyland met with the inspectors and gave evidence to them about his dealings with Traynor. Internal G&M documents showed that by the late 1970s O'Reilly-Hyland had loans of in excess of £600,000 which were backed by funds of equal magnitude in the Cayman Islands. O'Reilly-Hyland said: 'I certainly never hypothecated any of my trust funds to Guinness & Mahon, never, ever.' In other words, the backing was put in place without his knowledge. O'Reilly-Hyland said that any loans he got from G&M were backed by Irish-based security, and that that security was always adequate. 'They had no authority whatsoever to use my trust funds in the Caymans to secure any loans in Dublin or anywhere else because, Judge, this is meant as a hedge against Lloyds.' In fact, in the early 1990s, O'Reilly-Hyland withdrew £350,000 sterling from his trust account and used it as a part payment of a huge bill he'd received from Lloyds, which was then in difficulty.

The inspectors had a G&M document concerning a loan to a company, Beresford Investments, which had been signed by O'Reilly-Hyland, Traynor, Finnegan, McGonagle, Stephenson and Gibney. These were the six partners involved in the Fitzwilliam deal, according to O'Reilly-Hyland, who told the inspectors that he could not recall any company called Beresford Investments. The company which did the Fitzwilliam and other deals was called Marlborough Holdings. O'Reilly-Hyland said that Traynor would have been on the board of Marlborough Holdings as a representative of New Ireland Assurance, of which he was a director at the time. The inspectors found documents showing that GMCT had a 12 per cent shareholding in Marlborough Holdings, indicating that Traynor may also have been involved on behalf of the Cayman bank. The bank may have been, in turn, acting for a client.

O'Reilly-Hyland said that the background to the Fitzwilliam deal was that Goulding made the suggestion and then Stephenson and Gibney told Traynor that they could do a better deal. Finnegan was involved in assembling the site which would be swapped for the club's old premises. O'Reilly-Hyland said the Fitzwilliam deal was the only one he did with this particular syndicate. They didn't work together again for a variety of reasons, including clash of personalities, he said. The clash was not with Traynor, 'not at that stage', and it seems that it was not with McGonagle either. McGonagle was O'Reilly-Hyland's solicitor in the 1960s, and remained so up to the time of McGonagle's death in the late-1990s.

O'Reilly-Hyland said that he only once got a proper statement on his Cayman account between 1971 and 1994. That statement had come from Furze and it was wrong. However, he used to get scribbled memos from Traynor about once a year which simply stated what the balance was. Asked where this would happen, O'Reilly-Hyland said: 'I have met him in Guinness & Mahon bank. Very frequently he said, "I am having lunch in Jury's, that is where you normally have your lunch each day, so I will see you over coffee".' He twice visited Traynor in the offices of Cement Roadstone Holdings when Traynor later moved there. He used to store some of the slips of paper he got from Traynor in a tea chest in his boiler house and they got soaked in oil. Until the middle of the 1980s, he said, he did not know that the great investment team that John Guinness had spoken of was simply leaving his money on deposit.

By the early 1990s, Lloyds was in trouble and calling on its names for funds. O'Reilly-Hyland borrowed money from banks and took out some of his Cayman money, to pay off the London insurance firm. In early 1994 he went to see Traynor in his Cement Roadstone Holdings offices and told him that he wanted to close the trust. He was dissatisfied with how it was managed, and needed the money to settle bank debts and debts to Lloyds. Traynor closed the trust and O'Reilly-Hyland used it to pay off some debts. This happened in late March 1994, just weeks before Traynor was to die in his sleep. Members of O'Reilly-Hyland's family were also Lloyds names and also had debts settled.

Asked why he was unhappy with how the trust was run, O'Reilly-Hyland said: 'I had spoken to other people who had trust funds in London, there were trust meetings and my other colleagues would meet with the trustees. It wasn't just a question of a chap standing outside Jury's and saying, "you will know this, £312 in that", and putting it back.' In fact, when O'Reilly-Hyland went to close his trust account he and Traynor had different views over how much was in it. O'Reilly-Hyland thought it should be in the region of £400,000 while Traynor thought it was more like £240,000. Traynor was 'quite upset', according to O'Reilly-Hyland, and promised that he would sort it out in a meeting he was to have with Furze in the Cayman Islands. Traynor issued O'Reilly-Hyland with the balance that he, Traynor, thought should be in the account. Within a few weeks Traynor was dead and O'Reilly-Hyland was left not knowing if he had been swindled or not. During his interview with the inspectors in June 2000, O'Reilly-Hyland was shown another, legitimate withdrawal, for £160,000, which had been made from his account, and which he had not known about or calculated for when he had met Traynor in March 1994.

John Guinness was a keen sailor. So, too, was the young John Finnegan. In the 1960s he was an ambitious estate agent and a member of the Royal St George Yacht Club in Dún Laoghaire. It was through sailing that he got to meet John Guinness, and he sometimes stayed in the Guinness family home in Howth when he and Guinness were going to head off on an early morning sailing trip. Guinness invited

Finnegan to Guinness & Mahon bank for tea, and he got to meet Sir George Mahon. 'I was thrilled to be invited as I was a young estate agent in the commercial sector and these were merchant bankers, also in the commercial sector.' The bank had just been involved in a disastrous venture in Castleknock and Mahon employed Finnegan to sell his Castleknock home.

Finnegan knew Liam McGonagle and through him heard about Des Traynor. He knew Traynor was an accountant with Haughey Boland but also a board member of, and adviser to, some of the most successful private companies in the state. While still on the fringes of the Guinness & Mahon operation, Finnegan heard that the bank was taking on Traynor. Guinness told him that they were taking on Traynor so as to give the bank a 'commercial push'.

In time, Finnegan became more involved with the bank. At first he acted as estate agent in projects the bank had a stake in as well as financing. Later he began to have a stake in the deals himself. Traynor was always the central figure in so far as finance was concerned and he handled the distribution of the profits from the schemes as they matured. Just as he did with the others involved, Traynor suggested to Finnegan that he put some of the money he'd made into a discretionary trust. Finnegan agreed to the proposal and a trust was established in the Cayman Islands. The initial amount given to the trust was £200,000. That was in 1972. In 1973 he established a second trust, this time with Guinness Mahon Jersey Trust. It is not clear why, but it seems the money from this trust was later transferred to the Cayman trust. Finnegan told the inspectors: 'I have to say I was delighted and flattered to be getting advice from and giving advice to and participating with the likes of Liam McGonagle, Des Traynor, John Guinness and Guinness & Mahon. I felt that I was in very good company and Mr Traynor was regarded as Dublin's leading financial light at the time.' By the 1980s, Finnegan had loans totalling £1.8 million from G&M which were backed by offshore deposits.

Finnegan and McGonagle were particularly close, and were involved in a number of property ventures together. McGonagle's closest friend was Des Turvey and Turvey both assisted McGonagle in his business ventures, and for a time worked for Finnegan. McGonagle and Turvey grew up together, went to UCD together, attended each other's weddings and were generally very close. Turvey, an accountant by training who worked for various commercial companies, including Finnegan Menton, gave evidence to the inspectors about McGonagle, as McGonagle died suddenly in November 1999. Turvey said that from the age of ten, barely a day had gone by that he had not met up with his friend at some stage, often for a pint in the evening.

McGonagle was another yachting enthusiast. In 1973, he set up a company, Kinsale Yacht Charters Ltd, which owned or leased a 60-foot sailing boat for £40,000. It was used to sail around the coast of Ireland. Turvey was also keen on sailing and knew John Guinness from their joint membership of Howth Yacht Club. Howth was Haughey's yacht club and when his boat, the *Celtic Mist*, crashed on to rocks and was lost in the mid-1980s, it was McGonagle who spotted a boat for sale in Spain and suggested to Haughey that he buy it. The boat was purchased for £120,000 sterling in 1988, just after Haughey's return to power, and despite investigations by the Moriarty Tribunal the source of the money has never been discovered. The boat was later refurbished with financial assistance from the financier, Dermot Desmond.

McGonagle was also a member of the Howth club and he and Turvey sailed together for five decades. When McGonagle set up a trust with Guinness Mahon Cayman Trust in 1972, he told Turvey. He never told his first wife and he never told his second wife, Turvey believed. McGonagle worked from offices he owned on Molesworth Street. Turvey worked in the Finnegan Menton offices on Merrion Row and would regularly visit Guinness & Mahon on College Green. He would often conduct business for McGonagle while visiting the bank. Turvey helped McGonagle quite a bit and not for payment, although he did go on sailing trips abroad with his friend, which McGonagle paid for. McGonagle also put aside a significant sum from the money in his Cayman trust for his lifelong friend.

'He always thought he would die young. He used to say he would die before he was 40 or he would die when he was 50 because of his family history, and he always assumed that I would outlive him and that certainly that my wife, who was 14 years younger than me, would outlive him... So he left a substantial slice of the funds that were in the trust for me and my wife.' This would have taken place in the 1970s and the slice amounted to 15 per cent. Turvey regarded the money in the trust as, effectively, his pension. But the Ansbacher Deposits were discovered before Turvey could get the money.

Turvey said that McGonagle and O'Reilly-Hyland were the owners of the deal in Marlborough Street where they built an office block, Telephone House, which was leased to the Department of Post and Telegraphs. Once the tenants were in place, the pair sold on the property and made a huge profit. 'There were just the two there then and Liam's share of it was four hundred and something thousand pounds and that is the money that went to Cayman.' He said that O'Reilly-Hyland suggested to McGonagle that he become a Lloyds name and that he place some money in a trust just in case Lloyds came looking for everything he had. 'This all happened at a time before capital gains tax. There was no capital gains tax. So, that profit they made on that venture was not taxable and it was at the time when we were still in the sterling area so there was no breach of exchange control regulations. It was perfectly legitimate to do that at the time.' He said that Finnegan had large borrowings from G&M which were backed by offshore deposits. He was aware of both men's Cayman trusts and the fact that domestic borrowings could be backed by the offshore money.

Michael O'Shea, a solicitor in the law firm, Kennedy McGonagle Ballagh, and an executor of McGonagle's estate, told the inspectors that McGonagle was, 'an extraordinarily close, careful, prudent and secretive man.'

The Fitzwilliam Lawn Tennis Club deal was such a success that a number of the parties involved tried to repeat the trick, this time with the Kildare Street Club. The club owned numbers 1, 2 and 3 Kildare

Street and the consortium involved in this deal hoped that they could move the club and develop the three buildings. Number 1 is on the corner of Kildare Street and Nassau Street and currently houses the Alliance Française. The buildings beside it house the Heraldic Museum. On this occasion, two UK property developers were involved, John Lilley and Raymond Slater. O'Shea told the inspectors that McGonagle had a business relationship with the two men.

Lilley and Slater operated in Ireland by way of a company called Stonegate and did deals which McGonagle either was a part of, or gave advice on. The men also had an association with Finnegan. Stonegate began building up a stake in a UK property company called Norwest Holst, which had dealings in the Republic by way of a subsidiary, Rampart. In 1974, Lilley was appointed to the Norwest board and travelled to Dublin to take a look at the company's Irish deals.

One involved a plan to build a £1 million office block and shopping arcade in Drogheda. The second involved the Kildare Street plan. Norwest wanted out of these deals because it had cash flow problems and it extracted itself from the Drogheda one by giving a £50,000 termination of contract payment to the building company, Sisk.

Rampart had bought Number 1 Kildare St in 1971 and had then sold it on to New Ireland Assurance, the company Traynor was involved with. The club, New Ireland Assurance and Norwest thought that they could make more money from the remaining two buildings, and Rampart put down a £24,000 deposit. However, when the time came to close the deal, in 1974, both Norwest and New Ireland Assurance wanted out. Advice was sought by Norwest from McGonagle and Finnegan. It was agreed that the club would keep the deposit and be given a further £26,000 termination of contract payment. In other words, it had cost Norwest £100,000 to extract itself from the two Irish deals. McGonagle's law firm was paid £1,500 for its work on the matter. The firm's files on the Kildare St transaction were 'very small indeed'.

Later in the 1970s, two British Department of Trade inspectors were appointed to investigate Norwest because of concerns over certain share dealings involving the company. While making their inquiries, the inspectors noticed that the accounts for the year to March 1975 showed £200,000 having been paid in relation to the cancellation of the two Irish contracts, i.e. £100,000 more than should have been the case. They also discovered that the second £100,000 was paid by cheque to Guinness & Mahon in December 1974, and had been credited to a Cayman Islands company called British Isles Investments Ltd, which was managed by Guinness Mahon Cayman Trust. The inspectors decided to investigate the matter, and travelled to Dublin.

McGonagle, however, refused to meet them, citing legal professional privilege. Traynor told the two men that he could help them only to the extent that the interests of his bank's customer, British Isles Investments Ltd, were not compromised. He was not of much help.

According to the British inspectors' report, the Cayman company was part of a Cayman trust formed in 1971. No receipt or demand existed for the £100,000 payment and the cheque was given to Traynor. The inspectors were given two reasons for the transaction. One was that it was an under-the-table payment to a Norwest chief executive. The other was that it was a payment to McGonagle, or clients of his, for services in connection with the Drogheda and Kildare Street contracts.

Lilley told the British inspectors that he and McGonagle did business together in the Republic and sometimes holidayed together. He said that McGonagle was a 'fixer' of some renown and was 'not a solicitor in the ordinary sense of the word; he is a big developer.' Lilley said that the Cayman company was 'some kind of company that Mr McGonagle uses to handle fees and put deals through in probably the most tax efficient way to do it.' Lilley said McGonagle had helped in relation to another property deal, in Crumlin, Dublin, where there was a problem with planning permission. McGonagle, Lilley said, 'arranged for us to see the Prime Minister of Ireland, Mr Lynch, the next morning... That is the sort of power that Mr McGonagle has got. He is a real fixer, Mr McGonagle, there is no doubt about that.' Lilley also told the British inspectors that the Dublin business world was like 'a jungle'.

The inspectors wrote to John Furze and John Collins to ask them about British Isles Investments. Furze wrote back to assure them that the company had nothing whatsoever to do with anyone connected with Norwest. In a second letter, Furze complained that they had been visited by the fraud squad as a result of the Norwest inquiry. 'We have found this extremely distressing.'

The British inspectors decided to give no credence to what Furze had written and decided that the payment to British Isles Investments was an under-the-counter payment to Lilley and Slater (and not to the new Norwest chief executive). They also decided that the story about a payment to McGonagle had been made up by the two British developers to hide the fact that it was they who'd received the money. The Irish Ansbacher inspectors, nearly twenty years later, established that British Isles Investments was owned by McGonagle's personal trust in the Cayman Islands and was sometimes used for back-to-back loans from G&M. It seems that the British inspectors may have got it wrong.

6

Two of the Big Boys

J ohn Byrne, one of the largest customers of the Ansbacher operation over a number of decades, is a very successful property
developer who was a friend of Haughey's and who, during the
1960s, 1970s and 1980s, built office blocks which were subsequently taken out on long leases by the State. The nature of these
deals led to widespread suspicion that he was in cahoots with
Haughey in some improper way. In fact, Byrne was asked by
Seán Lemass and Sean McEntee to come back to Ireland from
England to build office blocks to house the expanding Civil Service.
Later, largely because of his relationship with Haughey, this arrangement got turned on its head, with the fact that leases were being
taken out by the State cited as evidence that Byrne was on some sort
of inside track because of the nature of his dealings with Haughey.

Byrne came from a poor background and grew to become a very
rich man who now lives in a large house in Ballsbridge on a number
of very valuable acres. He also has a large residence in his native
Kerry and used to keep an apartment in London, to which Charles
Haughey and his long-term mistress, the social diarist, Terry Keane,
went together on their first date. At one stage, Byrne flew his own
helicopter. He likes horse-racing and owns a stud farm in Ashbourne,
Co. Meath, close to where Haughey had his in the late 1960s.
According to a source, when Haughey, Byrne and a number of others
were at a dinner party once, Byrne mentioned in passing that he

owned every house on a particular exclusive street in London.

Byrne is very media shy. He was once approached during a break in the Moriarty Tribunal hearings and asked if he would do an interview for the *Irish Times* about his life story, if not his relationship with Haughey or the matters being investigated by the tribunal. He was friendly and pleasant but said no. 'Don't believe everything they say about me,' he added.

Byrne, however, had no choice but to give an extensive interview about his affairs to the Ansbacher inspectors. He also supplied a narrative statement covering his dealings with Ansbacher/GMCT. His relationship with the bank went back to 1971, making him one of the offshore bank's first customers. Byrne had begun to work with Des Traynor in the early 1960s and he was, of course, a Haughey Boland client. When Sam Field-Corbett left Haughey Boland at Traynor's suggestion and set up his secretarial services company, Management Investment Services, Byrne became a client of the new firm.

Byrne was born on a small farm in Co. Kerry in 1919. 'In 1941 I emigrated to England,' he told the inspectors in his statement. According to one source, Byrne got his first break when it was noticed how efficient he was at organising the clearing of bomb sites. 'I started out like many of my compatriots in construction and eventually built up a substantial building and property development business. I also involved myself in the development and operation of a number of dance halls and ballrooms in the UK, which were focused on the large population of young Irish immigrants in Birmingham, Coventry and London.' One of his larger ventures, the Galtymore, is still going in London.

'In the early 1960s, at the invitation of Seán Lemass and Sean McEntee, I decided to invest in Ireland and became involved in property development. My first property venture was the construction and development of O'Connell Bridge House on D'Olier Street in Dublin, which was completed in 1964. This development was carried out through Carlisle Trust Ltd, an Irish company originally incorporated and controlled by me. My second venture was the construction of an apartment block known as St Ann's at Ailesbury Road. This was also carried out through Carlisle Trust Ltd. My third venture was the development of D'Olier House (the former T&C Martin premises) through another Irish company originally incorporated and controlled by me, namely Dublin City Estates Ltd, in or about 1969. Although these ventures were carried out in Dublin, my principal activities were still being carried out in the UK.'

Byrne was also running the Mount Brandon Hotel in Tralee. The hotel was opened in 1965 by Lemass. A young rates collector there, Denis Foley, became involved in sourcing showbands for the dance hall in the hotel and in advertising and running the dances. He got a lot of his remuneration off the books and used the money to buy bank drafts, which he then kept in a drawer in a dresser at home. Occasionally, he would bring the drafts to the bank and exchange them for new ones, something he did not need to do as drafts, unlike cheques, do not go out of date.

Foley was good at his job and his employers, Byrne and two Kerry businessmen, the brothers Thomas and William Clifford, asked him to help run the dance hall in the Central Hotel in nearby Ballybunion as well. The top bands in the country played in both venues and Foley got on so well with his employers that he ended up going into business with them, getting a quarter share in the Central Hotel.

In the mid-1970s, Foley had what he described to the Moriarty Tribunal as a chance encounter in the foyer of the Mount Brandon with Traynor. The two men had tea together. Traynor seemed to think that Foley might have some money. 'What's your financial position?' he asked Foley. 'Because I'm with Guinness & Mahon now, and I'm in a good position to get you a good rate for anything you might want to invest.'

A few years later Foley decided to take Traynor up on his offer. He took the train up to Dublin and, with the drafts on his person, went to see Traynor in his G&M offices. Traynor took the drafts and said he would invest the money in something called Klic Investments. Over the years, Foley received occasional communications from Traynor as to how his deposit was growing. He also became a Fianna Fáil TD, but two decades after opening his account, his dealings with

Traynor became front page news and caused his political career to end in disgrace.

Following their encounter in the Brandon Hotel, Traynor grew close to Byrne and became a close and trusted adviser of his during the 1950s. 'I became very friendly with him,' Byrne told the inspectors. 'Anything I did I consulted with him. He was a remarkable fellow.' Byrne said that it was extraordinary how many people depended on Traynor. 'You know, you would be surprised – I mean there are times, you know, when you read the newspaper and it describes what they say and you would love to say something but, you know, you can't. He was the sort of man, Judge, that it doesn't matter what sort of a problem you had or worry you had. He had the capacity of saying, "Well, what are you worrying about, you know. It's nothing. I can solve that." He was like that.'

In 1961, the same year that Traynor and solicitor Christopher Gore-Grimes joined the board of the Gallagher group companies, they also joined the board of Byrne's Carlisle Trust. In 1971, when Traynor was establishing his Cayman bank, Byrne began to have dealings with it. He set up two trusts, one for his UK business and one for his Irish business. They were called, respectively, the Tristan and the Prospect settlements.

Byrne told the inspectors: 'By 1971 my business ventures in England were substantial and as I was becoming involved to an increasing extent in Irish property development, I was concerned to minimise my family's exposure to what was known then as "estate duty" in the event of my death. I took separate legal and taxation advice in Ireland and England from my respective advisors. I was advised that it was legally permissible both in Ireland and England to establish discretionary trusts domiciled and controlled in the Cayman Islands, which was at that time (1971) still part of the sterling currency area.

'Both trusts were founded in such a way that they are controlled by the trustees of the respective trusts. I received legal advice that the trustees of both trusts are under no obligation to accept any instructions from me in relation to the trusts. I have requested the trustees on a number of occasions to provide information to the

Moriarty Tribunal and they have not done so. Notwithstanding the above I am writing to the trustees requesting them to provide information to your inquiry... I do not control the trusts or the Cayman companies owned by the trusts. I do not have power to enjoy income from either.'

The relationship between Byrne and the trusts could be bizarre. Byrne had no right in law to tell the trust what to do, and doing so would threaten the tax advantages which accrued from having the assets held by a trust outside his control. In 1992 when Traynor asked him if he would invest in Celtic Helicopters, a company owned by Ciarán Haughey, Byrne said that he couldn't, that his Irish companies were not investment companies, or if they were, they were property investment companies. Traynor asked for permission to approach the trustees of the Byrne family trust and Byrne gave permission. Traynor, of course, was chairman of the Cayman bank which was acting as trustee. 'And that's what he did,' Byrne told the Moriarty Tribunal. 'And that's what happened. It was some time afterwards, a good time afterwards, that he informed me that he had and that I was the proud possessor of shares.'

The investment was £50,000. Byrne never saw the share certificates. The tribunal established that the shares were held by the Haughey family company, Larchfield Securities, which was in turn holding them in trust for Byrne. The whole matter was being managed by Sam Field-Corbett's company, Management Investment Services.

Byrne communicated with Ansbacher/GMCT by way of Traynor, and after his death in 1994 by way of Pádraig Collery. He had very little correspondence or documentation of any kind in his possession about either trust, he said.

The Cayman trusts owned Cayman companies which in turn owned other companies. The Prospect Trust and Prospect Holdings owned Carlisle Trust Ltd which in turn owned Byrne's other Irish companies. The Tristan trust and Tristan Securities Ltd owned Intramar Securities, a Cayman company which owned property in London, and Danstar Holdings Pty, an Australian Company. The directors of Danstar were Ron Woss, an Australian businessman, and

Pat McCann, an Irish accountant who worked for Sam Field-Corbett. Danstar in turn owned Tepbrook Properties Ltd, a UK company which owned property in London. The directors of Tepbrook were the same as the directors of Danstar. Why the Australian company was involved is not clear. Field-Corbett was involved in supplying company secretarial services to Tepbrook. Since the publication of the Ansbacher Report, Danstar has been removed from the Tristan trust structure.

In 1978, an Irish-registered company owned by Byrne, Breldorm Ltd, had dealings with the Gallagher group. The directors of Breldorm were Byrne, Traynor, and Anthony Gore-Grimes. Traynor acted as an advisor to the Gallagher group and had sat on the boards of Gallagher companies for years. Byrne was having difficulty getting a tenant for Seán Lemass House on St Stephen's Green. Eventually, the building was sold by Breldorm to the Gallagher group. Patrick Gallagher was head of the group by then, his father Matt having died four years earlier. The deal was the cause of some controversy in that Gallagher bought the building for £5.4 million and sold it on for £7.5 million just two months later. He sold the building on so quickly that he had only to pay a deposit of £500,000. The purchaser was the Irish Permanent Building Society and the deal was, at the time, the largest ever negotiated between two Irish entities. The principal negotiators were Patrick Gallagher and Edmund Farrell, with Farrell being the then head of the building society. He had inherited the job from his father and namesake and he later changed the name of the building to Edmund Farrell House.

In the early 1980s there was a political controversy involving one of Byrne's projects in Baldoyle, in north county Dublin. Another of his companies, Endcamp, had taken out a number of mortgages on sites in Baldoyle and Portmarnock in the mid- to late 1970s. Traynor was on the board of Endcamp and the company was planning to build two thousand houses between Baldoyle and Portmarnock. There was considerable local opposition, and Haughey was dragged into the controversy because of his known friendship with Byrne and Traynor. The controversy became so intense that Gore & Grimes

Solicitors issued a statement saying that it was not the case that Haughey had 'any direct or indirect interest, beneficial or otherwise' in the project.

The Moriarty Tribunal, during its public hearings into payments to Haughey, spent a considerable amount of time looking into the affairs of Prince's Investments, an Irish company which did not form part of the Carlisle Trust. Prince's Investments was the owner of the Mount Brandon Hotel, on Prince's Street, Tralee. The company's shareholders were Byrne and the two Clifford brothers, William and Thomas, who were also clients of Ansbacher Cayman.

In 1975, Prince's Investments took out a loan of £116,000 sterling from G&M and the loan was discreetly backed by money from the Ansbacher Deposits. Byrne and William Clifford were to later say they'd known nothing of the cash backing at the time. On 4 September 1985, the loan was cleared with a payment of £186,986 sterling. The money came from the Ansbacher accounts in G&M.

For two years after the loan had been paid off, false documentation was sent to Haughey Boland by G&M, purporting to show that the loan was still in existence. The documents were issued after Haughey Boland sought information concerning the loan as part of the preparation of the hotel company's annual accounts. It may be that the reason for the deception was to hide the fact that the company's loan had been paid off, in case the Revenue began to ask where the money had come from. Who organised the deceit is not known, though undoubtedly Traynor played a key role. One effect of the deception was that the company was entitled to claim the interest on the loan against tax.

On 23 July 1987, £260,000 was sent from Tralee, ostensibly to repay the loan. A cheque drawn on the Prince's Investments account in Tralee was used to buy what is called a banker's payment from AIB in Dublin, and that was then lodged to an Amiens account in G&M. Banker's payments are usually used by banks when one bank is making a payment to another. One effect of the use of the banker's payment was that when the tribunal sought to follow the money trail back from the lodgement to the Amiens account, AIB had to go on a massive trawl of its records in order to trace the payment to Tralee. Whoever had decided to use the banker's payment had been trying to break the money trail leading to Tralee.

Where the money went after it went into the Amiens account is not known. A similar scenario was discovered in relation to Central Tourist Holdings, the company which owned the Central Hotel in Ballybunion, and the directors of which were the Cliffords, Byrne and Denis Foley. The hotel was sold in 1986 and there was insufficient funds to discharge creditors. A settlement was negotiated between Haughey Boland, for the company, the Revenue, and G&M. The directors each contributed £7,000.

At the time of the deal, the loan the company had with G&M had already been paid off. It had been settled by a payment of £135,000 from the Ansbacher Deposits in September 1985. However, this was not known to the Revenue. When £42,000 was forwarded to the bank ostensibly to settle the debt, it went into the same Amiens account as the one the banker's payment had gone into.

Byrne told the tribunal that he'd known nothing of the repayment of these two loans at the time they were repaid and had not known of the backing given for the loans by Ansbacher. He had learned about it all for the first time from the tribunal and he had never given any consent to Traynor to conduct any of these transactions. It was all 'very mysterious' but, 'if it happened it happened', he said.

Haughey, when he was asked about the matter, said that he knew nothing about it and couldn't see what it had to do with him. Asked if he knew if Byrne had ever been approached for money for him, Haughey said: 'No. I don't think that he ever was and I think Mr Byrne has said from time to time publicly and definitely that he never subscribed personally to my finances, never subscribed to my personal finances at any stage. But I mean, I don't understand why these [...] I never heard of Prince's Investments in my life and I know nothing about these transactions. I just, when I saw them here in these documents as matters you were going to raise, I was baffled. Because I don't know or see how you can suggest that these had anything to do with me.'

Byrne, for his part, told the tribunal that although he had been a friend of Haughey's for forty years, he'd never given him 'a penny'. Asked why, he said: 'I just didn't.'

The inspectors told Byrne during his interview that they did not have pre-1990 accounts relating to his, Byrne's, Cayman affairs because Ansbacher would not hand them over. This meant that the inspectors could not get a full picture of his or the trusts' dealings with Ansbacher over the years. The documentation was not available to either the inspectors or the Moriarty Tribunal. Judge O'Leary, one of the inspectors, said: 'Of course you could make that information available to us if you wanted to, and you have chosen not to do so.' Byrne did not agree. The judge said Byrne could fire the trustees for not handing over the requested information. 'So it is disingenuous of you to say that you cannot get the information.'

Byrne said he had the same problem in relation to the Moriarty Tribunal. 'It has been a pain in the neck. So we decided well, there is only one way to solve this one. Get on the plane and head out to Cayman. We were getting nowhere. We made several attempts. We wrote several letters. We rang him up and they never responded to anything that we wrote. So we decided, well, we would go out there, more or less at the behest of the tribunal.

'Anthony Gore-Grimes and myself went out and we spent a couple of days there but we were […] there was plenty of chat and plenty of guff and plenty of everything else but there was no cooper-ation whatsoever. They said they would not cooperate whatsoever. They said they would not cooperate with the tribunal. No way they would. We employed a local barrister and solicitor to investigate the whole thing. He came back I think the following day or maybe a week after with his advice that whoever the trustees were that would be appointed, would be no better than the trustees that are already there. They still wouldn't provide the information and that is as […] so we came back with our tail between our legs.'

The matter was left to lie, though at the end of the interview the judge said that Byrne's answer was a 'disappointment' to him, and that he found it hard to accept that Byrne could not get the documentation if he wanted to. 'Judge, we thought really that we had done everything in our power to wrestle the documents out of them, and unfortunately we hit a sort of brick wall.'

From the early 1970s up to the discovery of the deposits, Byrne's Irish companies had significant loans from G&M, and later Irish Intercontinental Bank, which were discreetly backed by deposits from the Cayman Islands. From 1991 to 1997 the Irish companies took out loans totalling £17.5 million sterling which were backed in this way. During Traynor's lifetime Byrne would be given statements of his accounts from his friend, but after Traynor's death, when Pádraig Collery took over, he was not given statements, Byrne said.

He said that he had always considered the back-to-back loans to be a legitimate form of security for a loan. When he needed a loan he would ask Traynor and Traynor would set it up. In the 1980s this involved a curious role for Traynor who was at the same time a financial advisor to Byrne and a director of the company taking out the loan, the most senior executive in the bank, G&M, issuing the loan, and chairman of the Cayman bank which was acting as trustee for the discretionary trust providing backing for the loan.

The inspectors examined documentation in the G&M files relating to loans issued to Byrne companies. The facility letters issued by the Dublin bank made no mention of the Cayman backing which was in place. Byrne said this had never stuck him as odd or unusual in any way. He said these matters had been handled by Traynor. The judge asked Byrne whether, as an experienced businessman, did he not think that failing to mention the cast iron security which existed was a curious thing for a bank to do. 'Looking at it in retrospect I suppose you would have to think that way,' said Byrne. He said he would have been aware there was backing from the Cayman Islands for the loans.

Judge O'Leary said that some loans given to Carlisle Trust were backed by the Tristan trust, the trust which owned Byrne's UK business and which legally had no relationship with the Irish companies. 'You see, Mr Byrne, one of the conclusions that I have to consider and it is only one of the conclusions, is that this whole thing was a sham.' If the judge was to conclude that Byrne had control over the supposedly discretionary trusts, then this might breach the trusts' defence against Irish taxes. It could lead to a huge thirty-year tax bill from the Revenue to Byrne. Byrne said to the Judge: 'Well, all I can say, Judge, is that I took advice from the best people I could, as were available to me, and I was reliant entirely on them.'

In his statement to the inspectors, Byrne said that he never received any personal benefit from the monies held in the Cayman Islands. The judge then pointed to documentation which noted a draft for £3,500 sterling going from an Ansbacher account to Byrne.

The judge warned that he might come to the view that Byrne was entitled to access to the Cayman funds. Byrne said he had no recollection of the cheque and that he never knew he had access to the Cayman funds. His lawyers, Gore & Grimes Solicitors, later wrote to the inspectors saying that the amount was of no significance when compared to the scale of the funds held for Tristan Securities, and that there was no evidence that the cheque had been procured by Byrne.

An American Express card was being paid out of the 'J' memorandum accounts linked to Byrne, but Byrne said that he did not have such a card – he had a Diners card – and did not know whose card was being paid out of the accounts.

After considering the evidence available to them, the inspectors decided that Byrne, as against the supposedly discretionary trusts, had control of the funds in the trusts at all times. Before the report was concluded, Byrne's lawyers argued strongly that the inspectors were wrong to reach this conclusion and that it was unfair of them to do so based on the evidence available to them. Byrne's lawyers argued that it was wrong that Byrne should be placed in a position where he had to disprove the inspectors' view that the funds held by Tristan Securities in Ireland by way of Ansbacher were Byrne's to use as he saw fit. 'It cannot be the case as a matter of law that the onus of proof rests upon Mr Byrne to disprove this.' They also argued that the claim that the Cayman trusts were not under Mr Byrne's control was supported by the decision of the trustees not to release the files on the trusts to the inspectors, despite Byrne's request to them that they do so.

Ken O'Reilly-Hyland, in the top hat, getting ready for a hunt in the 1960s

Estate agent and property developer, John Finnegan, in June 1976

Sam Stephenson, architect, receiving an award from the President, Dr Patrick Hillery, in July 1986

Solicitor and property developer, Liam McGonagle

Charles Haughey and P V Doyle in Government Buildings in June 1980

Des Traynor at the CRH Annual General Meeting in May 1993

Charles Haughey, Minister for Justice, admires Joseph Malone's medal for services to the Lions movement in Jurys Hotel, June 1963

Denis Foley sporting a Jack Lynch sticker in the 1977 general election

Put Jack back!

The property developer, John Byrne, in Liberty Hall in 1984

Patrick Gallagher leaving the Moriarty Tribunal. He said in a newspaper interview that a group of businessmen agreed to bankroll Haughey in his political career.

John and Jennifer
Guinness

The Guinness & Mahon
building on College
Green, Dublin. The
bank's archives held the
key to some of the most
sensitive political secrets
of the Haughey era.

Tony Barry, chief executive of CRH, talking to Des Traynor at the company's 1992 Annual General Meeting

Brian Burke presenting his credentials as Ambassador for Australia to the Minister for Foreign Affairs, Brian Lenihan, and the President, Dr Patrick Hillery, in May 1989

Cork businessman and politician, Hugh Coveney, in the early 1990s

The inspectors' decision is likely to encourage the Revenue to vigorously assess the tax standing of the two trusts, opening the possibility of a tax bill of tens of millions of euro. Any such bill would be likely to be contested strongly by Byrne, and indeed, as this book went to print, Byrne was contesting the inspectors' findings in the High Court.

Pascal Vincent 'P V' Doyle was a private, hard-working, Fianna Fáil-supporting, Catholic church-supporting friend of Charles Haughey and Des Traynor, who became very rich through the successful hotel group which he founded and developed. He had dealings with the Ansbacher Deposits, but, unlike most of the rich people mentioned in this book, he did not have a trust in the Cayman Islands, preferring to stash his money in Liechtenstein.

P V Doyle came from a more privileged background than many of the other people gathered around Haughey, Taca and Fianna Fáil. He was born in Dundrum, Co. Dublin, one of seven children born to a farmer and builder. He attended Westland Row Christian Brothers School, the school attended by Traynor, but dropped out early. At the age of 22 he became involved in the construction business and in the 1950s he began to concentrate on hotels. He specialised in building new hotels in south Dublin, especially around Ballsbridge. He developed the Montrose, the Skylon, the Tara Tower, the Green Isle, the Burlington, the Berkeley Court and, finally, the Westbury, just off Grafton Street. He owned hotels in London, New York and Washington. In 1982, the hotelier, Colm Rice, reflecting on Doyle's career, said that Doyle 'recognised that there was a new affluent Irishman emerging – the kind of customer who on average would dine out once a week ordering, say, prawn cocktail, a steak (well done), fruit salad and coffee. P V went after him and they continued to do business in a remarkably expanding way. His insight was remarkable.'

In 1984, Doyle himself offered his view of what had happened. 'Dublin hotels were still catering for the ascendancy class,' missing out on the new emerging class of customers who were being created by the developing Irish economy. Doyle rose with his class, the Berkeley Court and the Westbury being the proof that this class had finally arrived.

Doyle's ability was widely respected. He was appointed chairman of Bord Fáilte in 1973 by Peter Barry of Fine Gael and remained in that position during a number of changes of government. He was a founder member of the finance committee of the Dublin Catholic Archdiocese, was a member of the board of the Meath Hospital, the Employment of the Blind Board and the Central Council of the Federated Dublin Voluntary Hospitals. He was a teetotaller but smoked, and he liked dancing.

Traynor was a close associate and advisor of Doyle's. Among the matters on which he contributed advice was the corporate structure of the Doyle group. Doyle had a number of companies in the US, including one called Extern, which was used to direct US people towards Doyle hotels when they were visiting Ireland. It was successful and a significant number of the high-spending US tourists who came to Dublin stayed in Doyle hotels. Every time Extern sent a US tourist to a Doyle hotel in Ireland, the hotel sent a commission to Extern. If the tourist stayed for one night, the hotel paid one commission; if the tourist stayed for three nights, the hotel paid three commissions.

Evidence was given to the Ansbacher inspectors by George Carville, a long-time associate of Doyle's and a senior executive within the Doyle group. Carville told the inspectors that in 1977 Doyle set up a Liechtenstein company which received commissions from Extern Travel. These commissions arose from the money which had originally been paid by Doyle hotels in Ireland, so, in effect, what was happening was that some of the money which the Dublin hotels were sending to the US was being transferred on to Liechtenstein. In time, these accumulated commission payments were transferred into a Liechtenstein foundation, or trust, called TAWA. This may have happened in the mid-1980s.

The whole matter was organised by Traynor, who helped the Doyle group put a US structure in place soon after Doyle began to acquire hotels there. Carville recalled Doyle saying: 'Look. We have to have some structure in America, and the best person to advise us is Des Traynor.' It is not known why Liechtenstein was used by Doyle in relation to his US operations, rather than the Cayman Islands. The use of European instead of Cayman entities meant that some of the monies which ended up in Liechtenstein had crossed the Atlantic twice.

Carville told the inspectors about meeting Traynor in relation to these matters. In 1981 Doyle rang Traynor and said he wanted to set up a structure in the US. Traynor said that he would be in New York the next week and why didn't Doyle or Carville come over and they could get advice from an accountancy firm there. Extern was already established, as was at least one of the Liechtenstein companies, but Doyle wanted to put an overall structure in place for his US operations. Carville went to New York. 'We went to one of the big accountancy firms and we told them our story... And how I remember it is, it is a bit funny if you don't mind, I remember when we were, believe it or not, in the toilets, and Des was a small man and he turns around to me and he says, "What do you think of that meeting?" and I said, "I am confused. I don't know. What advice?" He said, "They have given us no advice. Now," he says, "what we have to do is go back and tell them here is what we suggest we do. That we form a company for each hotel, have a holding company, and they will agree and they will charge you a few thousand dollars." And that is exactly what happened.' When Carville subsequently got a bill for $5,000 from the New York accountancy firm, he refused to pay.

The Liechtenstein trust became involved with G&M when the Doyle group took out a £1 million sterling loan to fund a new hotel in London in August 1983. The loan came from Guinness Mahon London but was backed with a deposit in Dublin in the Ansbacher accounts. The Dublin bank gave a guarantee to the London bank for the loan for 'cosmetic reasons'. When some of the details of the backing for the loan appeared in a draft Doyle Hotel Group set of accounts, Traynor spotted them and had them removed.

An Ansbacher account in Dublin was opened with a transfer from Liechtenstein. The Doyle group told the Moriarty Tribunal that this security was put in place by Traynor without the group being informed. It is not known what influence Traynor had over the assets held by the TAWA trust. A second account was opened to receive the interest earned on the Ansbacher deposit account. Statements on the account which received the interest were sent, on unheaded notepaper, to Carville after Doyle's death in 1988. The account used to back the loan was closed in late 1992 and the account used to receive the interest on the Liechtenstein deposit was closed soon thereafter. The latter account was closed as part of the re-organisation of the Doyle group's tax affairs, and the availing of the 1993 tax amnesty. It seems that the Doyle US holding company, IH Investments, also had a GMCT account in the Cayman Islands.

Carville explained to the inspectors that he was a bit vague on exactly what had happened in relation to TAWA because he didn't have any documentation. The documentation was held in Liechtenstein. The trust had been run by a number of people based in Liechtenstein with Doyle's main point of contact being a Dr Santa Passo, who worked in the law offices of a Dr Peter Marxer. The trust, it would seem, was operated with a similar level of secrecy to that which applied to the Cayman trusts, though perhaps with greater competence. No correspondence existed in Ireland, Carville told the inspectors. When they wanted to have dealings with the trust, Carville would travel to Liechtenstein and meet with Dr Passo. In January 1999, when the various inquiries into Ansbacher were under way, Carville travelled to Zurich airport and met Passo to get some of the basic details of the history of the trust. Passo brought his files to the airport and the two men discussed the matter there, but the files remained with Passo. Carville expressed the view that he wouldn't be able to get copies of the files from Passo for the inspectors.

Traynor's operation, because it allowed customers to gain access to their funds without any great difficulty, left lots of traces in Dublin. It was P V Doyle's use of Traynor for his 1983 loan which resulted in his affairs being dragged into the Ansbacher inquiry and details of the TAWA trust being printed in the inspectors' report. Other dealings he had with Traynor in the 1980s, involving Charles

Haughey, also left traces in the G&M archives, traces which were later examined in detail by the Moriarty Tribunal.

Haughey's two longest periods out of power were during the 1970s, after the Arms Crisis, and during the mid-1980s, when he sat in the opposition benches and watched Garret FitzGerald's coalition government run the State from 1982 to 1987. During both periods there is evidence that the flow of money into Haughey's personal coffers may have slowed. This is more so the case in the 1970s than in the 1980s. Haughey had a number of accounts in G&M during the 1980s, accounts which he said Traynor must have opened for him without his knowledge. The total lodged to these accounts was £1.7 million, though this total may involve some double counting with money passing through more than one account. It may also be the case that at the outset of the period Haughey got a £400,000 sterling loan from GMCT. If he did, then how this loan was settled is not clear, but there is no evidence of it being settled from Haughey's known accounts. The G&M archives show that much of the money that flowed into Haughey's accounts during the period did so by way of the Amiens accounts controlled by Traynor. The records for these accounts for the period, however, are missing. Sandra Kells of G&M said the files must have been removed, and that this was most likely done by Traynor or on his instruction.

However, he did not remove all of the Amiens accounts files for the period. The archives show that in May/June 1983, lodgements totalling £120,000 were made to one of Haughey's accounts from an Amiens account, with the money coming to that account from a loan taken out with G&M by P V Doyle. Carville told the Moriarty Tribunal that he had a vague recollection of Doyle telling him that he had guaranteed a loan to Haughey and that Haughey had agreed to pay it back. This instance of financial help is one of the rare occasions where Haughey later admitted knowing at the time that he was in receipt of money from a particular person. He said that Traynor told him in 1983 that Doyle was providing assistance. Why this was so he did not say. He also told the tribunal that Traynor had a policy of not telling him who was providing money for his, Haughey's, protection.

In 1985, Doyle took out another loan, for £50,000, from G&M, and again the money was drawn down in a number of tranches and used for Haughey's benefit. There is evidence to suggest that as well as taking out the loans Doyle may have paid the interest on them. In 1988, after Doyle's death, Traynor met with a number of Doyle's associates and told them about the loans and also that there was no chance that Haughey would ever pay the money back. Ultimately, the loans were settled out of Doyle's estate.

Part Three

Tales from the Ireland of
John Desmond Traynor

7

Seamus Purcell

Seamus Purcell was born in Birr, Co. Offaly, in 1922, the son of a farmer and cattle dealer, Pat Purcell. The Purcells, it seems, were a very hard-working family whose lives revolved around the cattle trade. Seamus and his four brothers, Michael, Kevin, Fintan and Albie, all mucked in to help their father from an early age. Seamus was on the road driving cattle at the age of five, and first started buying cattle at fairs when he was only 14 years old.

In time Seamus began to grow the family cattle-dealing business, and eventually he became a major force in the Irish live cattle and meat exporting sectors. He took time out from building up his business to hurl for his county team, something he did for 13 years. He kept fit all his life and used to say that you had to be fit if you were dealing at the sort of level he was. A day's work dealing with millions of dollars was as tough as a hard hurling match, he said.

He believed that his success was due to hard work and knowing his trade. 'We worked twenty hours a day if needed,' he told the *Sunday Press* in 1984. 'That was the way it was at home. You'd go to bed at eleven and be up again at one to go to a fair... The small farmers of Ireland would educate anybody when they went to a fair to buy cattle. I wish to God my children could get the education I got from those farmers. I would have no fear of them going into business if they had that background.'

Purcell met with the Ansbacher inspectors on 28 June 2000, and gave them a brief outline of his career. At the outset his lawyer made the point that Purcell was there involuntarily and under protest. Purcell said that he had started working in about 1937 with his father, buying and selling cattle and sheep in Ireland. 'Times were bad and there was a big family of us, about ten in the family. At that time then, after a few years, we started to earn a bit of money and I paid off our debts, my father's debts. Then when I had all that done, we had all that done, I started out on my own in about 1943.

'I looked after the family, all of the family, from there on until they all got big and went their ways. So, then, in about 1950, I started exporting to England and I worked there until 1970. Then, in 1970, in 1969/1970, I sent cattle to the Caribbean and to different places, Portugal and different places. Then after that I started shipping to the Middle East.'

In one year in the early 1980s, he shipped 317,000 cattle from Ireland. He did some barter deals, including one which involved a total of $155 million in goods. He set up deals involving sheep from Australia and cattle from Ireland. In the mid-1980s he bought some meat plants in Ireland and was soon killing up to 10,000 cattle per week. 'And we shipped every bit of that. We never put one bit of meat into intervention.'

However, it was not all plain sailing. When disease hit the Irish herd in the early 1960s he had to sell the home and farm he'd bought in Waterford. He built his business up again, but in the mid-1980s he got into trouble with the Department of Agriculture over the alleged double counting of cattle being loaded onto Purcell ships at Waterford. A fine of £3.65 million was imposed, but this was later reduced after a four-year court battle. The row hit his business hard. 'The Department held up a lot of (export) refunds on us and the banks came along then and looked for their money back. I owed the banks £49 million and $80 million in bonds. They came looking for every-thing so I had to sell all the assets and pay them and I paid them.'

The marts, he said, still trusted him and gave him credit and he managed to get his business going again. Then, in 1991, he gave the business over to his two sons, Gerard and Patrick. The business suffered another significant blow in the late 1990s when Gerard lost millions of pounds in currency speculation. Seamus Purcell, aged 78, pulled up his sleeves and went back to work to save his business once again.

Purcell told the inspectors about once introducing an Egyptian buyer employed by the Egyptian government to a man in the Waterford Castle Hotel. The man said: 'I suppose you know Seamus for a while', to which the Egyptian replied: 'I have good reason to know him. I have spent $270 million with him.'

Purcell's live cattle business, but not his meat business, was banked with G&M. The financial aspects of a large live cattle exporting deal could be complicated and at times Purcell had difficulty getting the banks to provide him with his requirements. In particular, he needed bonds which the banks would issue as part of the financial arrangements behind a deal where supply would take place over a period of time. Some time in the 1970s, a friend, a vet named Noel Hanley, suggested to Purcell that he try Des Traynor of G&M. Purcell got an appointment with Traynor, went to see him and explained what it was he needed. Traynor said he could supply the bonds. In return, G&M would take between a half and one per cent of the value of the bonds provided. The bank also issued Purcell with loans based on letters of credit Purcell received in the course of his exporting deals.

He was doing a lot of business with the Middle East, where large contracts could be landed with buyers who were working on behalf of governments. These people, or agents whom Purcell would have to act through, were sometimes paid commissions. 'In those countries at the time, in Egypt, you had to have an agent and that agent would get maybe two or three per cent on a contract.'

Purcell told Traynor that he needed a dollar account to pay these commissions, but Traynor told him that it wasn't possible to have one in Ireland. The banker said he would organise one for Purcell outside the State, but that Purcell would have to get him some dollars to open it. Legally, Purcell would have been allowed open a dollar account in the Republic if he could show why he needed it. However, some of the commissions he was paying were secret, and were outside or additional to the amounts due to be paid from the sales contracts. For this reason he couldn't go to the Irish authorities and show why he needed the dollars.

In 1981, Purcell said that he needed $1.1 million to go out to Egypt. He was under pressure but Traynor said it would take some time. 'Eventually I got it, the $1.1 million, but it held me up for [...] because President Sadat was shot and it held me up for about a month after, where I was looking for him to get my $5 million.'

It seems that it was after this experience that Purcell got Traynor to open a dollar account for him. Purcell was owned $450,000 from the sale of cattle to the Canary Islands. He got the money and gave it to Traynor. Traynor told him he would open an overseas dollar account for him. However, when he went to make withdrawals, Purcell got money from G&M.

'The first dollar payment I was able to get from that account was for $100,000, to one person outside. When I asked for that $100,000 they said no, we will give it from Guinness & Mahon, so they gave the $100,000. There was another one of $30,000 and there was another one of $50,000. That was all paid out by Guinness & Mahon at that time. There was maybe $100,000 here and there, I can't go back but I can remember a good few.'

Purcell said that Traynor did not make clear to him what was going on. 'Mr Traynor was a man you could not approach every day or ring up every day like that. At the time he was a great help to my business although he sold me a company that I had to let go bankrupt. The Wilson company. The pet food company. Maybe he thought it was okay but the books weren't okay.'

Purcell was sure the money from the dollar account came from G&M because he collected the money there himself. 'I went down to the bank myself and got a draft for $100,000. I went down and got cash for $30,000 and I went down and got cash for maybe $50,000 and I handled all those myself.' He was given the money into his hands and 'I gave it to the man who was with me'. This man was the person who was getting the commission payments. 'He wasn't an Irish citizen. He was from the Middle East.'

At the time Purcell owed $1.5 million in commissions. He paid all of this out of the account Traynor set up for him, even though only $450,000 had been lodged to the account by Purcell. Traynor may have organised a G&M loan for the balance. It seems that the need for secrecy only lasted for a short period, around 1982, and that it was then that Purcell dealt personally with the payments.

Later in the 1980s Purcell landed a few large contracts with Libya. At one stage, Haughey and Purcell travelled out to Libya to reopen that market after it had been closed to Irish cattle. This was a major breakthrough at the time for Purcell and for Irish cattle farmers.

During the same period, the mid-1980s, Purcell made a contribution to Ciarán Haughey's helicopter company, which was being set up with the help of Traynor. Purcell was in his offices when he got a phone call from Haughey, the then leader of the Opposition, asking him to meet with him for lunch in the Berkerley Court Hotel. Purcell went along to meet Haughey without knowing the reason for the meeting. The two men discussed the beef and cattle trade over lunch. When they were leaving, Haughey mentioned that his son was setting up a helicopter company and 'needed a bit of capital'. He asked Purcell if he would contribute £12,000 and Purcell agreed. Haughey told him Traynor would be in touch and the two men parted.

This request from Haughey is one of the few known instances of Haughey personally asking someone for money. Soon afterwards, Traynor contacted Purcell and asked him if he wanted shares in return for his contribution. Purcell said he did not. It seems no amount was discussed and when Traynor later transferred money from a Purcell account in G&M to an Amiens account where he was gathering contributions for Celtic Helicopters, he transferred £10,000 rather than the £12,000 which Purcell had agreed with Haughey.

8

Joe Malone

J oe Malone made a lot of money in the 1960s from the car hire company he set up and developed, Joe Malone Self Drive. He was a friend of P V Doyle and a friend of Charles Haughey. He was considered to be a key link between Haughey and a range of business figures and supporters in the commercial world. He served both on the board of Bord Fáilte and of Aer Lingus, and spent most of his working life involved in one way or another with the tourism sector. He also spent time on the board of the Smurfit group and worked for a US bus manufacturing company, General Automotive Corporation, or GAC.

Malone told the Ansbacher Inspectors how he met Des Traynor for the first time. In 1964 Malone sold his company to the Kenny Motor Group. Shell and BP were interested in the Kenny group taking on the franchise for oil and petrol sales. This involved getting control of a company called Dublin Petroleum, to which Traynor gave advice. Malone was going to try to buy out Dublin Petroleum from its owner, a man named Lanigan, on behalf of Shell and BP. Traynor came along with Lanigan to advise him in the negotiations. This, Malone told the Ansbacher inspectors, was how he and Traynor first got to know each other.

In the early 1970s Malone was working as the general manager of Bord Fáilte in North America. 'Ireland was much smaller then, you know, and there weren't as many people travelling to the States as now and it was a big deal. I met him (Traynor) at a function here in Dublin... He said he was going to the States and could I suggest a hotel he might stay at and I said, "Of course. I will make arrangements for you." So I made arrangements and he and his wife invited my wife and myself to meet with him and that was really the beginning of, you might say in the broadest sense, a personal relationship.'

During the meeting, Malone said that he had some assets back in Dublin and asked Traynor for his advice. The next morning Traynor called Malone. 'Joe. Would you like to meet for breakfast?' The two men met up the following day. Traynor said: 'You know if you are really interested in having someone look after your interests in Ireland, I would be very pleased to do it.' Malone said: 'That would be great.'

Malone had stocks and shares in Ireland. Traynor began to mind them for him using the G&M subsidiary, Mars Nominees. The shares were held in numbered accounts in the name of Mars Nominees, i.e. Mars Nominees number 6 account, or whatever. Traynor told Malone that he handled shares for a range of people, using Mars accounts. He also opened a non-resident bank account in G&M for Malone, who was non-resident as he worked in the US. A few years later Traynor asked if he could open a Cayman account for Malone. 'He said that G&M had a branch in the Cayman Islands, and that he was trying to build up his client portfolio, and would I allow him to do that. And I said yes.' At the time, Malone was coming back from New York. His Cayman deposit was coded A/G in the memorandum accounts.

Malone came back to Dublin in 1976 to take on the position of Director General of Bord Fáilte. He told the inspectors he had a salary of £12,000 a year, had £7,000 left after tax and had two daughters studying in colleges in the United States at a cost of £6,000 per year. Traynor, meanwhile, was managing Malone's portfolio of stocks and shares. 'He would buy and sell them. I had losses and profits because Atlantic Resources and a number of them didn't do well... and at that time the share market wasn't as buoyant as it is now.' After the Cayman account was opened the profits from the numbered share dealing account were lodged to the offshore account.

Malone said that he sometimes got loans of money from Traynor at short notice. He once needed £41,000 to give to AIB within three days and Traynor arranged it for him. On another occasion a member of his family got into difficulty in the United States, in Dallas, Texas. 'I went out to try and get bail and I was told that I had to produce $75,000 and I didn't know who to contact. So I called Des in Dublin and within two hours he transferred $75,000, not from my money, from G&M in Dublin.' He also got a number of substantial, five figure loans from G&M during the 1980s, loans which were secured by his Cayman funds. Malone told the inspectors that he had not known at the time that Traynor was putting this security in place.

The Cayman bank also held shares for Malone and it seems that when Malone's first account was opened in the Cayman Islands, his share dealing account was transferred from G&M to its Cayman subsidiary. The Cayman bank mostly used a company it owned called Overseas Nominees to handle share dealings, though Malone thought his shares might have been held in his own name. In 1988 Malone's account held the following shares in terms of value at cost: Aran Energy, £7,189; AIB, £88,324; CRH, £62,765; and Bank of Ireland, £6,765. At the time Traynor was the chairman of CRH. The total value of the shares, at cost, was £165,000. In 1985, when Malone moved back to the US to work and began to earn more money, he placed funds in the Cayman account and bought shares through his Cayman account.

Malone told the inspectors that he met John Furze twice. Once was when he was visiting the Cayman Islands to play golf with his wife and a number of US colleagues in 1988. Traynor suggested that he meet up with Furze, and he did so. He also met Collins at the same time, when they all had a cup of tea together, he said. The second occasion that he met Furze was at Des Traynor's funeral, in Dublin in 1994.

In 1985, when Malone moved back to the US, he began working with GAC, the bus building company. GAC had a plant in Shannon which built Bombardier/GAC buses for CIE. The plant was to have produced buses for export but it never landed an export contract.

Instead it built buses for the national bus company. The owner of GAC, US businessman Cruse Moss, made a small investment in Celtic Helicopters.

In the same year that Malone took up his new role with GAC, he was asked by Haughey, during a visit to Kinsealy, if he would chair the fledgling helicopter company that Ciarán was setting up. Malone declined to do so as he was at the time on the board of Aer Lingus, which had a helicopter subsidiary. He felt it would not be proper. Traynor, who was involved in organising capital for the new company, was also on the board of Aer Lingus.

During a subsequent visit by Malone and P V Doyle to Kinsealy, Haughey asked Malone if he would make an investment in Celtic Helicopters. Doyle and Malone discussed the matter after they left Haughey's house. Malone was concerned that Haughey might have been miffed by his earlier response to Haughey's suggestion that he chair Celtic Helicopters, and Doyle seems to have backed Malone in his decision to make an investment. Malone invested £15,000.

Malone told the tribunal that he believed that Doyle had also invested in Celtic Helicopters. Internal G&M records suggest that Doyle was indeed an investor. However, Haughey told the tribunal that he was 'as confident as I can be' that Doyle had never invested in the helicopter company. The hotelier's estate did not include any mention of a shareholding in Celtic Helicopters.

9

John Guinness

The Guinness & Mahon directors Sir George Mahon, John Guinness and Maurice O'Kelly (the former Haughey Boland accountant who joined G&M after Traynor took over) were all named in the Ansbacher Report as having been clients of Ansbacher. John Guinness lived in Howth with his wife Jennifer, and the couple became well known when a group of men kidnapped Jennifer Guinness and demanded a large ransom. She was held in a house in Dublin and seems to have built up a relationship of sorts with her kidnappers. It was said afterwards that they developed a great respect for her, and especially for her courage. After her release, Jennifer Guinness became an active member of the Victim Support group. In February 1988 tragedy again hit the family when John Guinness, out walking with his friends and wife on Mount Snowdon in Wales, slipped and fell to his death.

A short time after the tragedy, Jennifer Guinness was asked by Des Traynor to come to his office. Traynor and Jennifer Guinness had known each other since the 1960s and she considered him a personal friend. Traynor and her late husband were also close, both in terms of business and as social friends. At the meeting in Traynor's office, 'Mr Traynor spoke to me about John and while I do not recall his precise words, the gist of it was that my late husband John had established a trust for me and my children and that the trust was administered in the Cayman Islands.'

The news came as a surprise to her, though she knew that GMCT existed because her husband and Traynor had travelled to the islands. 'You have to understand that my husband was a banker, a merchant banker in the old fashioned sense of the word and confidentiality meant confidentiality. He never really discussed business affairs with me. I used to get a bit cross with him at times but he wouldn't discuss any business matters with us at all.' Traynor told her very little about the trust. 'He sort of indicated that if I needed money to spend, I could ask for it... but it wasn't money to be used day-to-day in Ireland. It was money to spend on holidays, airline tickets and that sort of thing. I wasn't to assume that I could just draw down on a regular basis money to use in Ireland.'

When she needed money she would telephone Traynor. 'I would say, "Des, look, I am going to Australia," or "I am going to" wherever and he would say, "fine"... It was never in cash, it was always traveller's cheques... I remember going into CRH and collecting traveller's cheques.' Sometimes she had money transferred to an account with Barclays bank in London. After her husband's death she decided to go on a sailing trip around the world and she used trust money for this.

'After my return permanently to Ireland, I saw Mr Traynor from time to time and on many of these occasions he showed me statements which gave the value of the trust. At some of these meetings I expressed general unease about the trust, I think, on reflection, because of a nagging worry about taxation and also because I had no real knowledge of the workings of the trust and no control over it or of the funds in the trust.' She was shown statements but not given them. She was never given any documents relating to the trust and nor did she ask for them. Most of the assets were US and UK stocks and shares.

She said that she developed concerns about the taxation aspect of the matter. 'It was a little bit cloak and dagger going to collect traveller's cheques... I just believe if you live in a country you should pay your taxes. Life is much less complicated if you pay your taxes in the country you live in, like paying VAT on boats and things. It is much easier if you pay your tax, then you don't have to worry.'

'When the (1993) tax amnesty was announced it provided me with the opportunity to regularise my affairs and Mr Traynor agreed to assist me in this. He instructed Don Reid to act on my behalf. Mr Reid is a tax expert of whom I had heard but had not met. Mr Reid made returns to the Revenue and entered into negotiations with them on my behalf.' Settlement was reached and a payment made. Reid, of course, was the man who had given advice to Traynor and G&M about GMCT in the 1970s. Guinness had very little contact with him in relation to availing of the amnesty, and it seems that it was all arranged between Traynor and Reid.

Guinness was one of the executors of her husband's estate. The trust was not declared to the Revenue at the time. She was not clear, she told the inspectors, if she was told about the trust at the time the estate was being administered or afterwards. 'I don't think I really realised the trust funds had anything to do with the estate in Ireland.' Her solicitor at the time was Liam McGonagle. Immediately after John Guinness's death some of the Guinness family tax affairs were dealt with by Sam Field-Corbett's office.

It took her a long time to question what was going on, she said. 'I suppose I didn't question because these were, as far as I was concerned, very reputable people who had been friends, and it is very hard to believe that the person, I mean banking was a very respectable profession and it is very hard to believe that people aren't as straight... I do remember the tax amnesty coming up and the huge relief that now this was going to be easy to deal with.' When the assets from the trust were repatriated, the stocks and shares were transferred from Cayman to her account with NCB stockbrokers, 'because we had fallen out with Guinness Mahon, I had no more accounts with Guinness Mahon.' She never received any documentation concerning the closing of the trust, she said.

10

The Cork Connection

T rading in Atlantic Resources shares is a subject which is mentioned in a number of places in the Ansbacher Report. The oil company prospected for oil in the Celtic Sea during the depressed 1980s, and there was intense punter interest in its shares. Speculation about the company's prospects was rife and the share price would shoot up or down depending on the latest rumour. In 1983 the company had something of a crisis when, during a shares issue, its shareholder base failed to take up all of the new shares being issued. As a result, the bank which underwrote the issue, the state-owned ICC Bank, was left holding £3.5 million worth of unwanted Atlantic stock.

Just a month later, in July 1983, the Atlantic shares jumped in price, from 43p to 105p, on the back of rumours concerning a block – an area on the seabed – the rights to which were one-third owned by Atlantic. The US group, Gulf Oil, was drilling in the block and when it confirmed that it had found oil the Atlantic share price leaped to 190p. During the following nine months there was intensive speculation in the shares as investors awaited confirmation that the block held commercial quantities of oil. But it didn't, and by the time the fact was made public by Gulf Oil, in April 1984, a lot of small investors had lost out. One person who didn't lose out, however, was David Doyle, son of P V Doyle, who placed the profit he made from Atlantic Resources in a G&M account opened for him by Des Traynor.

Three Atlantic directors, Vincent Ferguson, Jim McCarthy and Neil Collins, used Ansbacher-related entities to secretly buy Atlantic shares during this period. The inspectors were told that the three men organised a loan of £1 million to buy shares which were still being held by ICC Bank. The shares were bought in the period between the first and second announcements by Gulf Oil. McCarthy said they got the loan from Traynor because the main banks would not loan money for the purchase of speculative shares. Furthermore, McCarthy's other business interests were in difficulties and the banks would have known about this.

Traynor organised the purchase of the shares by way of a nominee GMCT company called Medford, with the money coming from GMCT. Asked why he chose to invest so much money, McCarthy told the inspectors: 'It was simple, you were involved in a drilling programme and like every redneck on the rig, you knew what was happening.' He told them that the offshore company was used to distance the true owners from the share register, i.e. to hide their identity. He also conceded that if they had made money there 'would have been a gain which would have been enjoyed by a company offshore and that might have presented a tax opportunity.'

There was no opportunity, however, for the three men because when the second Gulf announcement was made the shares they'd bought at 102p per share dropped in value to 65p per share, and were soon down to 60p. The men were paying interest on their £1 million loan at 10 to 12 per cent and were pretty soon, as Ferguson put it, 'under water'. Traynor helped them refinance their debt to GMCT. They bought more shares, including some in Fitzwilton, a company Ferguson and McCarthy were directors of, and which owned part of Atlantic. The second round of investments was another failure and the men were soon under severe financial pressure. Collins had to liquidate many of his assets to settle with Traynor. His difficulties dragged in his brother, Dr Patrick Finbarr Collins. The two men had been left a substantial amount of shares from an uncle, Con Neenan, who had built up a fortune selling Irish Sweepstakes tickets in the US. Dr Collins lost some of his assets, which he had entrusted to the care of his brother, as a result of the Atlantic debacle. He was himself named as an Ansbacher client.

McCarthy and Ferguson were friends of Tony O'Reilly, the Heinz chairman and controller of Independent Newspapers, who was then the chairman of Atlantic and Fitzwilton. Both men were on the board of Independent Newspapers. O'Reilly agreed to guarantee the two men's debts and take over the payment of interest. In 1997 McCarthy's debt was cleared with a gift of £1 million from O'Reilly's wife. A year later, O'Reilly honoured his guarantee in respect of Ferguson. The extent to which O'Reilly knew what was behind the difficulties encountered by the men is not clear.

Neil Collins was unfortunate in that he was twice cited in the Ansbacher Report, and on both occasions in relation to disastrous commercial deals. Collins was a businessman who ran Heffernan's Travel in Cork, and was also heavily involved in property development. He told the inspectors that when he was given his inheritance of money and shares by his uncle in the US, he was advised by Stokes Kennedy Crowley that it would be more productive to invest the assets offshore. He set up a trust with GMCT to hold funds for both himself and his brother, Dr Patrick Finbarr Collins.

Collins was also involved in something called the Lynbrett Trust, a GMCT trust set up as part of a property deal involving a 90-acre trailer park in Arizona. There were five people involved in the deal: Neil Collins, Clayton Love Jr, Hugh Coveney, Pat Dineen, and Frank Boland. They were all Cork businessmen who engaged in projects together, as well as running their separate careers. Each of the Corkmen had a Cayman company assigned to them by Traynor and all of the companies were in turn owned by the Lynbrett Trust. The deal came about by way of Jim Cummins, an Irish-American who used to holiday in Cork. He suggested to Collins and Boland that they get involved in the Arizona deal along with him and two other US businessmen. The US businessmen could secure tax advantages if 50 per cent of the deal involved non-US investors, and in time the five Cork investors became involved.

Collins got onto AIB in New York about their putting some money up for the deal. A study was undertaken which concluded that the park could yield a profit of up to $10 million. Traynor gave advice on the structures that should be put in place. AIB put up $2.77 million and the five men had to provide personal guarantees. The five Corkmen also had to put up $950,000 and they divided this input between them. Hugh Coveney's input was $212,500, or 22 per cent.

Coveney gave an account of the venture in writing to the Moriarty Tribunal prior to his death in 1998 from a fall while out walking by the sea. 'Despite the attractive projections and extensive due diligence carried out by AIB and ourselves, the enterprise ultimately turned out to be an unmitigated disaster and an absolute nightmare for the other Irish participants and myself.' On 18 February 1986, AIB called on the five men to pay a debt of $2.57 million within 30 days. 'A protracted and publicised dispute followed between AIB, their lawyers and ourselves, which was ultimately settled out of court in late 1993.' Collins could not pay his share and it had to be paid by the others, each of whom had to pay $500,000.

Hugh Coveney was an avid sailor. He opened a GMCT account in 1978 when he sold a yacht, the Silver Apple, in the US for $193,508. When the money was withdrawn, in December 1979, it was used to buy a new yacht. Coveney's son, Simon Coveney TD, has said that it is his understanding that no tax had to be paid on the proceeds of the Silver Apple and that there was no evidence that the account had been used to evade tax. The dealings involving the US trailer park made a huge loss and so no tax issue arose.

In June 1979, when his GMCT account was still in existence, Hugh Coveney put himself up as a Fine Gael candidate in the local elections. He was first elected as deputy for Cork South Central in June 1981. He was Lord Mayor of Cork in 1982, and was appointed Minister for Defence in 1994. He died on 14 March 1998. The day before he died a letter was sent out by the Moriarty Tribunal containing evidence that it had discovered an Ansbacher account which belonged to him. He had already given his full account to the tribunal concerning the trailer park deal. The letter concerning his account arrived at his home on the Monday after his fatal fall.

Joseph Clayton Love Jr was a director of G&M. His father, Clayton Love Sr, ran the family business, the Clayton Love Group, which, among other activities, traded as ship's chandlers, fish processors, general wholesalers, restaurant operators and frozen food distributors. In the latter capacity the group handled the distribution of Findus Foods in the Republic. By the 1950s the group was doing well and expanding and Clayton Love Sr decided that he needed a larger firm of accountants. He ended up opting for Haughey Boland, who nominated Traynor to handle the account. Traynor impressed the Cork family and was appointed a director of the group of companies in the late 1960s.

Clayton Love Jr, who had a difficult relationship with his father, left the family business in 1969. He discussed the matter with Traynor before making the move. After leaving he became a director of a number of companies and also became involved in property development. Traynor was a trusted advisor and Clayton Love Jr became a non-executive director of G&M in 1969, at the invitation of his sailing friend, John Guinness. Guinness was hoping to get more business from the Cork region, and a branch of G&M was opened in Cork.

Clayton Love Jr told the inspectors that he set up a Cayman trust in April 1971, on the advice of Traynor, to protect some of his assets should all of the personal guarantees he had given be called in. His accountants at the time were Haughey Boland. Love received regular statements on his Cayman accounts from Traynor. Traynor also told Love that he could borrow from the trust, which Love did, though in a surprisingly informal way. Nothing was put down in writing and there was an oral agreement between Love and Traynor as to the rate of interest which would be paid. Up to the time of his giving evidence to the inspectors, in March 2000, Love had repaid no interest or capital on loans taken out in the 1970s. He only did so after being interviewed by the inspectors.

One of the companies Clayton Love Sr had as part of his Clayton Love Group operation was a food distribution company called Clayton Love Distribution Ltd. Dublin businessman, John Mulhern, was involved with this company as managing director since its establishment in 1966, and became a 55 per cent owner of the company in the 1970s. Mulhern, who is married to Charles Haughey's daughter, Eimear, told the inspectors about the background to his involvement in the company as a shareholder.

In 1972, he explained, he became the 55 per cent owner of the company, with Nestlé taking the other 45 per cent. The company distributed Findus Foods, which were owned by Nestlé. In time, both sides wanted to buy each other out, but neither side wanted to sell out. The price put on the 45 per cent stake was £300,000. It seemed like a lot of money at the time 'but when you look back on it now, it was a pittance,' said Mulhern. There seemed to be no hope of resolving the situation until Des Traynor became involved and suggested a solution.

'The situation was that we had spent a day in the solicitors and we were getting nowhere. I was to report to him (Traynor) in the evening and I reported to him that we hadn't made any progress. He said, "If I may join the meeting, I will progress it." So he came to the meeting and said, "My client doesn't want any more legal bills, he doesn't want any more of this stress. The only solution is that we will name a figure. You can give us 45 per cent of it and you can have the company or we will give you 55 per cent of it and we will have the company".'

Mulhern said that he was surprised by the suggestion and had no idea who was going to put up the 45 per cent. 'It all happened in half an hour.' When Mulhern questioned Traynor after the meeting, Traynor told him that a company called College Trustees would hold the 45 per cent. College Trustees is an offshore G&M subsidiary based in the Channel Islands. College Trustees got the 45 per cent and, Mulhern told the inspectors, he did not know who they were holding it for. Traynor said it was all right and that was good enough for him, he said. He rejected the suggestion from the inspectors that it was his, Mulhern's money in College Trustees that was used to buy out Nestlé. He said that he would send a set of accounts to Traynor every year but was never told who owned the 45 per cent. He did not believe it was Traynor himself. Sam Field-Corbett was appointed to the company's board as a representative of College Trustees.

In 1992 Waterford Foods expressed an interest in buying Clayton Love Distribution Ltd. Mulhern told Traynor and Traynor said: 'If it's suitable to you, College Trustees will accept it.' Mulhern did not go ahead with the deal but, he said, the negotiations brought it to Traynor's attention that the company held a lot of cash, £1.5 million. No dividend had ever been paid to the 45 per cent owner. Traynor now suggested to Mulhern that the company buy back the 45 per cent with its cash reserves. 'You won't have any outsiders to worry about, you can do what you like with the company,' Mulhern said Traynor told him. The £1.5 million in the company was used, and a further £1 million-plus was borrowed from National Irish Bank. College Trustees got £3.2 million back on its original investment of £300,000.

During the interview, Mulhern said that he'd received a £750,000 loan from Traynor in 1992, and had not agreed a rate of interest. The money came from an Ansbacher account in Irish Intercontinental Bank, but he said that he had not known this at the time. When asked what the agreed interest rate was, Mulhern replied: 'In those situations, sir, you don't concern yourself with the agreed interest rate when you are dealing with somebody who you have known all those years and who has been your godfather... You don't query the interest rate, you know you won't be robbed.'

Mulhern said that Traynor had given him a lot of help over the years. 'On many occasions in other years involving other deals or transactions you would go to him and say, I want to do this or that. He would say let me think about it. Two or three days later he would ring you and say, "Go and see David Went in Citibank. Go and see Gerry Tierney in Northern Bank Finance". And when you went in the thing was done... All you had to so was sign.'

The College Trustees shareholding was bought out for £3.2 million with the money being paid over in two tranches, £1.42 million and £1.77 million. Mulhern's solicitors wrote to the inspectors after

Mulhern had been interviewed and told them that the £1.77 million had ended up going to Mulhern. In other words, he got more than half of the money that was paid for the 45 per cent. The money was paid into a bank account in AIB Jersey in February 1994. The account was in the name of a Jersey-registered company bought 'off the shelf' by Traynor for Mulhern's use.

Mulhern strongly denied that he was an Ansbacher client, but the inspectors decided that he was. They said that the way he had dealt with the College Trustees issue 'called into question the extent to which the inspectors could rely on Mr Mulhern's evidence.' They concluded that loans secured by Mulhern from Traynor, and which were discovered by the inspectors to have come from the Ansbacher Deposits, came from offshore funds owned by Mulhern. It is not known who got the rest of the money paid for the College Trustees stake in the distribution company.

11

Drug Dealers and Australians

In January 1990, lawyers acting for the US authorities wrote to John Furze in the Cayman Islands concerning the G&M nominee company, Mars Nominees Ltd. In its letter, the US authorities informed him that Mars had been listed on a Drug Enforcement Administration computer and advised him that if the company conducted any future transactions in the US, it was possible that these transactions would be considered suspect. Seven years before the discovery of the Ansbacher Deposits by the Irish authorities, the US authorities had considered a key G&M company to be suspicious.

The reason the US authorities harboured suspicions about a merchant bank on College Green, Dublin, was because of the dealings it and its Cayman Islands subsidiary had had with a Cuban national and convicted drugs smuggler, Fernando Pruna, and his associates. During the late 1980s the banks had loaned Pruna more than $3 million.

Fernando Pruna was born in Cuba in 1935, the son of a prominent Havana lawyer. He attended private schools in the US and worked for a number of Canadian mineral firms before returning to Cuba in 1957. He was elected to Cuba's House of Representatives but, following the Communist revolution, he was arrested as a political prisoner and sent to prison for 20 years. He escaped from prison and joined an anti-Castro resistance movement fighting in the hills of

Pinar del Rio. In 1959 he was captured, accused of being a CIA agent and sentenced to death by firing squad. The sentence was subsequently commuted to 35 years imprisonment. When he was released in 1980, after serving 17 years, Pruna was allowed go to the US, where he got a job with an investment bank in Miami. However, within a year, he began drug trafficking with his brother, Andres Pruna, and before long the two brothers had built up a very substantial and profitable drug smuggling operation. In 1985, while Pruna was running a marijuana smuggling operation based in Miami, he began to do business with GMCT, and his business grew further when he branched out into the more lucrative cocaine market.

One of the key elements in the Pruna operation was the involvement of four crooked customs officers. One of these officers was a pilot who ran radar and drug-spotting planes, supervising night patrol flights from Florida. Another ran a customs unit at Key Largo, and another was in charge of an enforcement division in New Orleans. Information provided by these officers to Pruna allowed him and his colleagues to avoid detection when they were spiriting drugs up from South America and into the US by way of the coast of Florida.

The authorities eventually rumbled Pruna. When they swooped in October 1989 they charged 19 people with smuggling four tons of cocaine into the US since 1981. Pruna fled to Argentina, using false documents, around the time of the swoop but was brought back to the US following a four-year extradition process. In 1993 he was sentenced to 12 years in prison for drug trafficking and for attempting to bribe a witness.

Pruna smuggled drugs from Colombia, moving them via the Bahamas and Belize. The Cayman Islands, of course, is in the middle of this territory. By the time his ring was broken up, it was using Cessna aircraft to carry out marijuana drops, mother ships and fast boats from the Bahamas and a refuelling station in Mexico for his drugs vessels. Pruna's assets were discovered to include a 140-acre ranch in Texas, aircraft, and expensive jewellery. Arresting FBI officers seized three freighters, five smaller boats, a plane, $54,000 in cash, and property worth $500,000. As part of an international investigation the Dutch authorities seized a 120-foot vessel. And then there was the Cayman/ Irish connection.

Between 1985 and 1988, G&M issued loans of more than $3 million to Fernando Pruna and his wife, Edulia. These loans were secured by deposits in G&M made by GMCT, and the customers were introduced to the Dublin bank by the Cayman subsidiary. Loans were also given by G&M to a company associated with the Prunas. The bank had trouble getting the gangster to make interest repayments.

In time, the bank took further security on the loan, using a property in Dade County, Florida. The title of the property was transferred to Mars Nominees. In June 1988, when there was an outstanding balance of $700,000, the Dublin bank was repaid from the deposits of its Cayman subsidiary.

Soon afterwards, the US authorities were busy trying to track down property owned by Pruna. The Dade County property was still in the name of Mars Nominees. In March 1990, a judge in Florida issued a request to the Irish courts for co-operation in relation to an investigation of alleged organised crime and drug smuggling by Pruna. In November 1990 the High Court in Dublin ordered officials in G&M to attend court to be examined on oath. It is not clear who attended to give evidence.

The US authorities concluded from their inquiries that Pruna and his gang had used several bank accounts at G&M and its Cayman subsidiary to deposit profits from their activities, and to facilitate the movement of profits from drugs smuggling to bank accounts located in countries throughout the world.

The first two loans to Pruna and his wife were issued by G&M in 1985. They were for a total of $395,000 and were backed by Cayman deposits. In December 1986, the bulk of this money was replaced by a loan to Raymond G Fitzgerald, and two years later all these loans were settled.

A loan of $2.1 million was subsequently issued by G&M to a company called Northside Management and Development Company, of Atlanta, Georgia. The loan was secured by a guarantee from Maxima Investment Corporation, a company of which Pruna was the president, and a Channel Islands company. It was also secured by a deposit of a similar amount by GMCT.

In 1985, a loan of $75,000 was advanced by G&M to two associates of Pruna, Jesus and Maria Barrios. This loan was also eventually discharged from backing deposits. Ms Sandra Kells of G&M told the Moriarty Tribunal that at the time Furze might have been using the Dublin bank's name without its permission or knowledge. It may have been the case that Furze, while moving money for Pruna, only made it seem as if the transaction had involved a loan from the Dublin bank.

It seems that Furze may also have lied to the US authorities about the matter. In a letter to US lawyers in December 1989, Furze said that a property owned by Pruna had been transferred to Mars Nominees 'unbeknownst' to him. However, documents later discovered by the Moriarty Tribunal indicated that it was Furze who had suggested to Pruna that the property be transferred and had then organised the transferral. In the same letter Furze asked if any action could be taken to distance Mars from Pruna, as G&M had become concerned that Mars had become tainted through its association with Pruna. The US authorities wrote back to say that Mars Nominees had been listed on the Drug Enforcement Administration's computer.

In the story of the Ansbacher Deposits, the cameo role played by Pruna is unique in that he is a straightforward crook. The links between the Ansbacher Deposits and Australia, however, involve a more familiar cast of characters: business moguls and a dodgy politician.

Central to the story is Brian Burke, the one time Premier of Western Australia, who, following his fall from grace, served for a time as ambassador to the Vatican and the Irish Republic before having to return home and face the music. Shorthand descriptions of Burke and why he troubled people bear an uncanny resemblance to the scenario with Haughey. Furthermore, both men had Traynor helping out with their finances.

Burke's forebears came from Co. Clare and his wife's came from Co. Tipperary. His father was a Labour Party member of the Australian

Federal Parliament from 1942 to 1955. Burke started out as a print, radio and television journalist, but was elected to the Western Australian legislature in 1973. Ten years later he was elected as Labour's first Western Australian premier in a decade. Three years afterwards he was re-elected premier, the first Labour party leader to win consecutive Western Australian polls in three decades.

His regimes, however, were noted for controversial links between politics and business, with the controversy centring around payments by business figures to Burke and his party, Burke's use of this money, and efforts by Burke's governments to support the business figures who'd made these donations. A key figure in all of this was Laurence (Laurie) Robert Connell, the chairman of a merchant bank, Rothwells, and the son of an Irish emigrant bus driver.

Connell was one of the brash and extravagant entrepreneurs who prospered in Western Australia in the 1980s. He built his bank from the shell of a Queensland menswear retailers until it was a multi-million dollar business involved in backing some of Australia's most successful businessmen, as well as being involved in joint ventures with Burke's government. Connell was Burke's key link with the business-men who funded his political career. Burke once said of Connell: 'I wouldn't like to be standing between Laurie and a bag of money.'

Connell's fame in Australia in the 1980s rested, among other things, on his having once won AU$3 million in a single horse-racing bet. He was known to keep a large number of expensive racehorses, and to live a hugely extravagant lifestyle. However, after the stock market crash of 1987, his bank found itself in severe difficulties.

The truth was that his bank had always been insolvent, a fact not, however, reflected in the bank's books. Money invested in the bank was apparently Connell's to spend as he wished, which is what he did. The stock market collapse led to a run on the bank and a situation which not even the most creative of accountants could conceal. Burke and another business supporter, the former tycoon Alan Bond, tried to save Connell's bank. They pumped AU$570 million into the effort. As part of this effort, the Western Australian government and the Bond Corporation paid Connell AU$350 million for his half-share of a company called Petrochemical Industries Company Ltd. A year later, in 1988, the bank collapsed. That same year Burke resigned and was appointed Ambassador to Ireland and the Holy See. He moved to Dublin where he kept a low profile and began to socialise with, among others, Des Traynor.

Back home in Western Australia, the clamour was growing for some sort of inquiry into Burke and his government's links with big business. An inquiry into how millions of Australian dollars could have been wasted on Connell's bank led to the creation of a more broad ranging inquiry: the Royal Commission on Commercial Activities and Other Matters. It became known as the WA Inc Royal Commission. Burke resigned as ambassador and returned to Australia to deal with the commission.

In 1992, during his testimony to the commission, Burke said that he had received £200,000 in an interest-free loan from a Dublin businessman. The businessman was soon identified as Des Traynor. Burke told the commission that he'd received the money between February 1989 and January 1991, i.e. when he'd been living in Dublin. Traynor's name was mentioned in the Australian federal parliament in relation to the loans, which it was said were used to buy property, silver, crystal and cars. Traynor, when asked about the matter by the *Irish Times*, described Burke as a very good friend who, he said, was 'under pressure on a continuous basis from the bank'. That was the context in which the loan was given, he said. He said the amount involved was £129,000, and was given in two loans, and that £80,000 had been repaid. It was a rare instance of Traynor speaking to the media.

Traynor also said that he had met the commission during a visit it made to Dublin and had appraised it of the exact situation. Asked if he had business dealings in Western Australia, Traynor said that he was aware of how business was done in Western Australia, and that he would have nothing to do with it. It seems he was not telling the truth. The commission never got to the bottom of what was going on. When it issued its findings in October 1992, it said it had come to no conclusion about the loan, as it had been unable to interview Traynor.

In December 1991 an Australian accountant working with the commission sent a fax to IIB bank in Dublin. He was investigating matters to do with the collapse of Rothwells bank and wanted to know more about a payment of £91,000 sterling made on 20 February 1991, through the Royal Bank of Scotland in London, from an account in the name of Ansbacher Cayman.

IIB, which had just begun to do business with Traynor and Ansbacher, knew nothing about Rothwells or Laurie Connell. An official contacted Traynor about the matter and a month later Traynor got back to the bank to say that he was dealing with it. He gave IIB a copy of a letter he said he was sending to Australia. In the letter, Traynor said that he was disturbed that the Western Australian Crown Solicitor's Office, where the accountant worked, had contacted a Dublin bank with the details of a transaction concerning a Cayman bank, given the confidentiality which surrounded the dealings of Cayman Island banks. He also said that, despite Cayman secrecy laws, his client had agreed to co-operate with the Australian authorities. Who exactly his client was in this respect is not clear, but the indications are that Traynor did not co-operate with the commission.

During the 1980s and 1990s, the Ansbacher Deposits were used regularly for the transfer of funds between Australia and the Cayman Islands, with the funds moving via Dublin. As well as Connell, another prominent Western Australian figure known to have had dealings with the accounts was Ron Woss, the Australian business-man who served on the boards of two companies belonging to one of John Byrne's Cayman trusts.

Woss, the chairman and major shareholder in a publicly-quoted Australian technology company, Tennyson Holdings, used an Ansbacher account to organise the buying and selling of shares in Australian companies up until the establishment of the McCracken (Dunnes Payments) Tribunal in 1997. Woss was a well-known figure in Perth business circles, who was once investigated and charged by the tax authorities in Australia in connection with a so-called 'bottom of the harbour' scheme. These were schemes which were popular in Australia in the early 1980s, and which involved the owners of companies which were facing large tax bills selling those companies to intermediaries, who then destroyed the companies records so as to make it impossible for the tax due to be collected. In some cases the records were scattered at the bottom of Sydney Harbour, hence the name given to the schemes. Woss was cleared of the charges brought against him.

The Ansbacher account used by Woss to buy and sell Australian shares was called the Diamond Trust A/A26. Instructions in relation to the account came from Woss or from John Furze in the Cayman Islands. After Traynor's death in 1994, Sam Field-Corbett, who by this time was housing the Ansbacher files in his offices on Winetavern Street, Dublin, became more involved in running the Diamond Trust account on a day-to-day basis. Instructions would come in a few times a week, the Moriarty Tribunal was told, and would in the main involve the transfer of funds to Australia. Once the McCracken Tribunal started to investigate the Ansbacher Deposits, the account became dormant.

Woss did not respond to the inspectors' requests for information about the account. They interviewed Field-Corbett about the matter, and he said that he did not know who owned the Diamond Trust account. He took instructions in relation to the matter from Traynor up to 1994, and after Traynor's death from Furze. He said Woss told him that he did not own the account and he thought it might have belonged to Furze. 'Ron Woss was the advisor and he has, actually, told me it is not his and the only fellow left is John Furze.'

Judge O'Leary: 'Why would Mr Furze be using Ireland to get involved in buying and selling shares in Australia? That would not make any sense.'

Field-Corbett: 'I have only conjecture on that point.' The conjecture was never asked for. During the interview it was disclosed that one payment made in relation to the account in 1994, soon after Traynor died, was for AU$295,000. The account was a very active one over many years, and after 1994 Field-Corbett would file weekly reports to Woss in Australia about the state of the account. The inspectors decided that the account belonged to Woss.

Woss would make a number of trips to Ireland each year in connection with the accounts and other business interests. He was a director of the British-registered company, Tepbrook Properties, which invested in a shopping centre in the London suburb of Cricklewood. Field-Corbett was another director. Filed accounts for the company in 2000 showed that it had tangible assets of £8 million sterling and retained profits of £807,251. Tepbrook was, in turn, owned by the Australian company, Danstar Holdings Pty Ltd. It had the same address as Tennyson Holdings, the quoted technology firm whose board Woss chaired. Woss was a director of Danstar, and its two issued shares were owned by Furze and his Cayman Islands colleague, John Collins.

The WA Inc commission investigated a number of deals entered into by the Burke government, including the purchase by the state in 1993 of a company called Northern Mining, then owned by the Australian entrepreneur, Alan Bond. Northern Mining's main asset was a 5 per cent stake in the Argyle Mine, the largest diamond prospect in the world. It was alleged that the state had paid AU$15 million over the odds for the stake by buying Northern Mining in a deal put together by Connell. The stake was bought by Western Australia Diamond Trust, a semi-state company. It is not clear if the Diamond Trust account in Ansbacher was in any way linked to these dealings.

In the wake of the commission's report, Burke was charged and tried for taking public money under false pretences. The case concerned expenses claims for trips already paid for. The crime was uncovered by the commission in the course of its investigations. Burke was sentenced to three years in prison. An interesting aspect of the overall affair is that the WA Inc commission, despite the fact that it had to investigate a number of very complicated deals, sat for just 18 months. Within a year of its report, Burke was charged, tried and jailed. The Moriarty Tribunal, which is investigating payments to Charles Haughey and Michael Lowry, was established in 1997 and is still in existence. Also, at the time of writing, no politician has yet been convicted of any offence uncovered by the series of inquiries and revelations which began in 1996/1997.

As well as uncovering the expenses fraud, the WA Inc commission heard that millions of dollars were raised by Burke for the Labour Party from Australian business figures. Burke's estimate was that $8 million Australian was raised. Some of this money was used by Burke to make investments in gold and rare stamps. This activity continued after his resignation as Premier and appointment as ambassador to the Irish Republic.

In February 1997, Burke was the subject of a second set of convictions, this time in relation to seven counts of theft from the Labour Party. The total amount involved was £60,000 and Burke was sentenced to jail for three years. Again, the money had been used to buy stamps for Burke's stamp collection, with some of the valuable stamps being bought from Connell. During the trial, Burke said that the stamps were being collected as an investment for the Labour Party. In July 1997 Burke's conviction on this matter was quashed on appeal. One of the issues raised during the appeal was whether the Labour Party had legal title to the money raised by Burke.

Connell died in February 1996, aged only 49, and while in the process of fighting charges of having falsified his bank's accounts. Bond's business empire has collapsed and he has spent time in prison. When asked in 2001 about his connections with Traynor, Burke said that he had no intention of discussing the matter. His name did not feature in the Ansbacher inspectors' report.

12

Neighbours

Des Traynor lived in Kilronan, a large Victorian house with substantial front and rear gardens on the Howth Road, Clontarf, Dublin 3. The six-bedroomed house was doubled in size in a project designed by the architects, Stephenson and Gibney, which was carried out soon after the Traynors bought the house in 1970. They had five sons and one daughter when they moved in, and a sixth son was born afterwards. The house was designed with the holding of parties in mind, having an unusually large reception hall with a high ceiling from which a cut glass chandelier hung, and four reception rooms. Lots of parties were held there over the years. At the end of the reception hall, through double doors, was Traynor's book-lined study. He had a period-style desk and a door leading straight out to the back garden, where there was a tennis court, a vegetable patch, and a two-roomed coach house.

Upstairs, the main bedroom ran the width of the front of the house. Again there were double doors leading into the large room, which had a walk-in dressing room and a bathroom with a separate sauna. The gardens and house were surrounded by high walls and there was an electronic security gate.

Just as Haughey regularly held meetings in the library of his house in Kinsealy on Saturdays and Sundays, so, too, did Traynor hold meetings in his study. Haughey's son-in-law, John Mulhearn, himself an Ansbacher depositor, told the *Sunday Business Post* in 2002, that

119

Traynor would be available to callers on Saturdays in his Howth Road home. It was like 'confession', Mulhearn said. People from the upper echelons of the Irish business world would go to Traynor and tell him what was was troubling them. No problem, Traynor would say, and suggest a solution.

A number of Traynor's neighbours ended up in the Ansbacher Report. Sean McKeon, of 160 Howth Road, a property developer, had a trust established in the Cayman Islands in 1986. He and his partner, John Kennedy, ran the building company, Sheelin Homes. He told the inspectors that he remembered a conversation with Kennedy and Maurice O'Kelly, of G&M, where O'Kelly suggested the creation of a trust. (Kennedy also set up a trust) When McKeon set up his trust, O'Kelly introduced him to Traynor and to Pádraig Collery. Unheaded statements on the account were sent to his Sheelin Homes offices. He closed the account in January 1994, just before Traynor's death, in order to settle with the Revenue as part of the 1993 tax amnesty. In the run-up to the closure he met Des Traynor at the Cement Roadstone Holdings offices on Fitzwilliam Square a number of times.

Brian Dennis, a long-time friend and neighbour of Traynor's, also had a Cayman trust. Dennis was a successful businessman who ran H B Dennis Motors, as well as a car rental firm, a car financing firm and other related businesses. He lived two doors away from Traynor and the accountant acted as both confidante and advisor to Dennis. Dennis already had a trust with the Bank of Ireland, but following discussions with Traynor in the early 1970s he used after-tax money to create a second one in the Cayman Islands. The money was to be used when his sons got married. When he needed money from the trust because a son was getting married, he would get the cheque from Traynor during a meeting in Traynor's home. The trust was closed in the late 1980s. The inspectors discovered a cheque from Dennis to Traynor, dated 1993, and asked Dennis about that. It was for a mutual friend of theirs who was in financial difficulty and had nothing to do with the Ansbacher Deposits, Dennis said. 'Mr Traynor organised help amongst the friends'.

During a conversation in the 1950s with an employee in Frank Glennon & Co, insurance brokers, Dr Thomas Killeen mentioned the fact that he and his wife, Ita, also a doctor, did not have an accountant. The doctors ran a general practice on Mountjoy Square dealing mainly with working class, medical card patients. They were advised to try Des Traynor, in Haughey Boland, the man who did the insurance company's accounts. (Francis Glennon was to end up with a substantial amount of money lodged in an Ansbacher account.) Dr Killeen went along to Haughey Boland, and Traynor set up a simple system for him for keeping the books. There were three columns on a sheet, with fees earned in one, fees banked in the next, and fees not banked in the third. By the early to mid-1960s the doctor had lost contact with Traynor. However, when the Killeens moved to a house on the Howth Road in June 1977, they found that Traynor was their next-door neighbour, and so the two men became friendly again.

Ita Killeen did midwifery work, including work in a nursing home on the Howth Road. She did a lot of charity work with Fr Michael Cleary. 'He used to have a whole lot of these poor unfortunate girls that he used to collect and she used to deliver them in St Anthony's Nursing Home in Howth Road. One of these girls wanted to keep the baby and we were short a domestic at the time, so we offered to take this girl and the child, which we did. As time went on, Des Traynor had a young son who was a similar age to this youngster that we were looking after, and they used to go in next door, and one Sunday they were in next door and they were blowing into Des Traynor's dogs' eyes and one of them bit this youngster. This would be about 1982 or 1983. Mr Traynor came in and was very upset about this and we arranged for the child to be taken to Temple Street Hospital and stitched.'

Killeen used to call in to talk with Traynor on occasion. Shortly after the incident with the dogs, he and Traynor were in Traynor's study in his home and were talking about banks. Traynor said that his bank, G&M, would give a better rate of interest than Bank of Ireland, which Killeen was using. 'So I started to pass some money over to Des Traynor.' Killeen thought that the money was being placed in an account with G&M on College Green, though he never visited the bank. Lodgements were made in Traynor's study, and were usually cheques or cash. Killeen was still using the bookkeeping plan outlined by Traynor in the 1950s, and the money he now started to give to Traynor came from the fees earned but not banked column. (Though not banked, the income was declared to the Revenue.) Every quarter or half-year, Traynor would slip a beheaded bank statement in through the Killeen letter box, showing the state of Killeen's account and the interest which was accruing.

It was a very informal way of doing banking business. Killeen knew that Traynor was a very significant figure in the Irish banking world as well as in the business community generally, but he did not wonder why such a person was, in effect, acting like a messenger boy for him. 'You see, we looked after him medically. I was his family doctor and he was a man that was not very well, and we looked after him fairly well... I honestly thought I was the only one that he was doing this for and he was only doing it because I was his next door neighbour. This is the reason and I had no reason whatsoever to think otherwise. Absolutely none at all... When you come to think of it, boy, was I naive, wasn't I? My goodness.'

In the 1980s there was enormous media coverage of the fact that the broadcaster, Gay Byrne, had invested much of his money with an accountant who had spent it all but concealed the fact from Byrne. The truth only emerged after the death of the trusted accountant. The story made Killeen a bit worried and he began to ask Traynor a few questions about his account. When he asked Traynor where his money was, Traynor said that it was in the Cayman Islands.

'Now, this bothered me. We have a banker friend who lives in America and I spoke to this gentleman about the situation. He said to me, "I will come back to you." He came back to me after two months and he said, "You have no money in the Cayman Islands". This bothered me.' After a few months, Killeen broached the subject with Traynor. 'Des, where is all this damn money?' Traynor said it was in England.

Killeen was reassured by this. He was doing well in his practice and had an aeroplane. It needed some repair work and he asked

Traynor for a sterling cheque. It was delivered. 'Any time I asked for a cheque to get the repairs done, if they were large sums, I gave him two to three days notice and a cheque would be organised for me.' Some time in the 1990s, Traynor gave him a letter saying that he, Traynor, was retiring as chairman of Ansbacher. It was the first time that Killeen realised that he had money with Ansbacher bank. Traynor said he could take no more money from Killeen, but he continued to facilitate withdrawals. 'Practically all that money went on looking after our aircraft.' The money lodged to the account was declared income, but Killeen never paid tax on the interest. After the deposits were discovered, Killeen had Pádraig Collery close his account and he used the money to settle with the Revenue. He described the situation as a 'debacle'. He said he had had complete confidence in Traynor and that was why he had trusted him so much. 'My confidence in him is shattered now.'

Barbara Breen was a senior executive with Merops (Nutrition) Ltd, a pet food company. She was a personal friend of Traynor's and lived close to the Traynor family. Traynor's wife, Dofeen, had baby-sat for her when Breen was a child. When she'd bought a house in Ireland in the 1970s, she had taken out a loan from G&M, because, at the time, building societies rarely gave loans to women. Jack Stakelum was on the board of Merops and when Breen was buying a house in Portugal in 1980, she discussed the matter with him. The house was bought in the name of a Cayman company supplied to her by Traynor, called Coral Reef Securities Ltd. Furze was a director of the company. It was organised so that in the event of the simultaneous death of her and a friend, Thomas McLaughlin, the property would be disposed of on the instructions of either Traynor or Stakelum. McLoughlin owned Merops, and Traynor, it seems, made it his business to ensure that McLoughlin looked after Breen.

At some stage, McLoughlin set up a fund with Traynor which was to be used by Breen. 'It was something which was there if the roof fell in,' Breen told the inspectors. It had nothing to do with tax evasion, she said. It was a personal matter involving money being put aside in case she ever needed it. She said that Traynor had asked McLoughlin for the money. 'It was Mr Traynor who asked Mr McLoughlin for this money in order to take – to look after me if something happened to him or whatever.' The initial amount was £380,000.

Breen's solicitor told the inspectors that he had spoken to McLoughlin about it before McLoughlin died. 'It was Des Traynor who approached him. He didn't know Traynor at all well... Mr McLoughlin had sold some shares in the early 1980s for a substantial sum of money and had used the stockbroking services of Guinness & Mahon to do that. He then shortly afterwards received an approach from Des Traynor who rang him up and asked him to meet him in the Shelbourne Hotel, which he went and did, and Mr Traynor said that effectively on behalf of, almost like as if *in loco parentis*, he was asking for a fund to be put aside for Barbara because she had no pension and she had been working in the company for 16 years.' There was no question, the solicitor said, that tax was owed on the funds left with Traynor.

According to Traynor's son, Tony, Traynor would visit Haughey most Saturdays, and sometimes also on a Sunday. Haughey's personal secretary in Leinster House, Catherine Butler, who would often go to Kinsealy at the weekends, told the Moriarty Tribunal of meetings in the Abbeville library which were attended by Traynor and other business acquaintances of Traynor and Haughey. The weekend visitors were usually business people rather than politicians or civil servants. At the weekends, Haughey would often dine in Johnny Oppermann's restaurant in nearby Malahide. Traynor and his family also frequented the restaurant and became friendly with Johnny and Eileen Oppermann. Some time in the 1970s, Oppermann asked Traynor for advice on a good place to invest and Traynor replied: 'If you have any money, give it to me and I will invest it for you.' The Oppermanns began to give Traynor regular amounts of money, £300, £400, £500, and Traynor took it with him. 'We never at any time asked him where the money was. We used to get from him now and again a little piece of paper with just how much we had invested with him and what amount of profit we had made on it... Let me say this to you. We had so much confidence in that man that we never queried at any time.' At one stage they cashed in some government bonds and gave £35,000 to Traynor.

Most of the money Oppermann gave Traynor was after-tax salary, and so there was no tax issue. However, 'on occasions, he had a dinner party in the restaurant, we will say, which was not very often and he [Taylor] would say, "Look, I will lodge that to your account".' These lodgements, therefore, were untaxed deposits. The Oppermann's told the inspectors that they did not know where their money was, even whether it was in Ireland or abroad, until contacted by the Moriarty Tribunal. When the Oppermanns were making withdrawals they usually got the money in traveller's cheques or in cash. They collected money from Traynor in G&M, and later in his CRH offices. Sometimes, Traynor even delivered money to them at their restaurant in Malahide.

Part Four

Chairman of the Board

13

Number 42
Fitzwilliam Square

By 1986, Traynor's regime at G&M was drawing to a close. The Central Bank was making noises about auditors' reports and extending the exercise of its supervision to GMCT. Around the same time, the Dublin bank sold its subsidiaries to its London parent. The funds from the sale were used to improve the health of the Dublin bank, which had been hit by a number of bad debts. The sale also had the effect of taking the Cayman bank out from under the responsibility of the Central Bank. Around the same period, Traynor announced his decision to leave the Dublin bank. This announcement was noted in a Central Bank report arising from an inspection conducted in February and March 1986. Traynor resigned after having a bust-up with some of the executives in London, seemingly in relation to a major loan which had worked out badly.

Traynor stayed on in his role in the Cayman bank. Although he had been a major force in the bank since its inception in January 1971, he was not officially a director of the bank between 1974 and 1981. It seems that he was not officially a director in case it would have tax implications for the bank. In 1981, the Cayman bank passed a motion to the effect that Traynor's duties would be performed solely in the Cayman Islands 'and the authority of the appointee to act on the company's behalf is limited accordingly'. The Ansbacher inspectors decided that the official absence of Traynor from the Cayman board during the late 1970s was a legal fiction, and that he was at all times a director of GMCT. Of course, Traynor spent half his working life working for the Cayman bank in Ireland, irrespective of any resolution passed in the Cayman Islands in 1981.

When Traynor left G&M in March 1986, the bank came to an agreement with him as to how he would continue to operate the Ansbacher Deposits. He was given an office in Trinity Street, in the building owned by the bank, and moved there along with his secretary, Joan Williams. He was given use of a computer which was linked to that in the College Green premises. Memos from Traynor and Williams flowed from Trinity Street to College Green, telling executives about withdrawals, lodgements, transfers and orders for cash. Memos also went from them to Pádraig Collery, so that he could make the necessary adjustments in the secret memorandum accounts. Traynor and Williams received some remuneration from the Dublin bank for a twelve-month period after they left. The Cayman business was a key part of its operations and the bank was anxious not to lose it.

A year or so later, Traynor went to see Dermot Desmond, of NCB Stockbrokers, and told him that he wanted to move his nominee share dealing accounts from G&M. Desmond agreed to take the accounts into NCB Stockbrokers. The accounts were in the name of the Cayman company, Overseas Nominees, and when they went on the NCB books they were placed in the name of an NCB company, Aurum Nominees. In other words, the first Overseas Nominees account, when placed with NCB, would be given the name Aurum Nominees No 1 account, and so on with each new account. So the shares would be bought in the name of Aurum Nominees No X account, and the entity Aurum was buying for would be a numbered Overseas Nominees account. The first account moved was that of Charles Haughey, though Desmond didn't know this at the time.

Meanwhile, Des Traynor was, as always, busy. In April 1986, Michael Dargan, the chairman of CRH, announced his intention to resign from the position. Traynor, who was on the board of CRH, was immediately appointed deputy chairman. The appointment was equivalent to being appointed chairman designate. In May 1987, Dargan formally tendered his resignation and by unanimous resolution Traynor was appointed to replace him. The board knew nothing of Traynor's falling out with G&M, or the fact that a disastrous loan which had hit the bank hard formed part of the backdrop to Traynor's departure.

Cement Roadstone Holdings was, at the time of Traynor's appointment, one of the great successes of the Irish business world. It was an indigenous manufacturing company which was developing into an international force, the type of business that the Irish Republic needed if it was to ever become a first division Western economy. It was one of the state's top five companies, and was at times during Traynor's reign the number one company in the state. In 1987, CRH had a turnover of €916.2 million and a market capitalisation of €433.26 million. These figures doubled and tripled respectively during Traynor's time as chairman. It was not for nothing that he was so highly regarded.

Traynor was an active chairman, taking part in the deliberations of a number of key committees. He left the Trinity Street offices and moved to the CRH chairman's offices at 42 Fitzwilliam Square, Dublin. He worked from this address for the rest of his life, from upper floor offices in a Georgian building. Once again, Williams came with him. Traynor attended the office daily, arriving early and before most other members of staff, and staying until mid-afternoon. Approximately two days a week were spent on CRH business, while the rest of his time was spent on his many other business interests. It was the beginning of a new chapter in the history of the Ansbacher Deposits.

Like so many aspects of the upper echelons of the Irish business world in the 1980s, the roots of CRH went back to the opening up of the economy under the general stewardship of Seán Lemass. The company was formed from two separate Irish companies, Irish Cement Ltd and Roadstone Ltd, and the merger of the two came about in part because of the desire of the government to prevent Irish Cement from being taken over by the English company, Readymix. It was considered important that the state have its own, indigenous, cement company and that the production of such a key material should not be under the control of foreign boards. The squeeze was put on the two companies by the government through Irish Life, a state company which had significant shareholdings in both Roadstone and Irish Cement.

The initiative for the merger came from Roadstone, which was fed up dealing with the problems caused by industrial unrest in Irish Cement Ltd. In 1970, Irish Cement was closed down by a dispute which lasted a number of months. Tom Roche, who had built up the Roadstone company, decided to bid for Irish Cement. It was an audacious move given that Roadstone didn't have the money to buy Irish Cement, a gilt-edged, cash-rich company, which at the time had the only licence for the production of cement in the Republic. Roche offered shares in Roadstone instead of money. Readymix then jumped into the fray, offering to buy Irish Cement. Irish Life Assurance then became involved. It had a 10 per cent stake in both Irish companies and, acting on pressure from the government, it in turn pressurised the two Irish companies to merge. When the merger went ahead it proved difficult. There were four representatives from each company on the board, and the chairman was Seán Lemass. When he died he was replaced by Roche as non-executive chairman.

The problem was that the boards of the two companies were not particularly keen on the merger or, more to the point, were concerned about who was going to end up being top dog after the merger, Irish Cement or Roadstone. There were some very strong personalities involved and there were boardroom rows and even, it seems, boardroom bust-ups. Traynor played a key role in making the whole thing work and was a director of the company from its inception. Lemass was chairman of the company from 1970 to 1972. Haughey, when he was thrown into the political wilderness by the upheavals of the Arms Crisis, was considered as a possible successor, but the idea did not get off the ground.

CRH bought 17.5 acres in Kinsealy from Haughey in December 1973, when Haughey was entering one of the more difficult periods of his financial career. The price paid was £140,000, almost the same price that Haughey had paid in 1969 for his Gandon-designed mansion and 240-acre estate. In March 1999, CRH issued a press release saying that Traynor had had no role in the transaction and that the land purchased was prime, limestone-bearing land. Whatever about being involved or not being involved from the CRH end, there can be little doubt but that Traynor was involved from Haughey's end of the deal. There is no way Haughey could be involved in such a deal without Traynor taking charge of the details. The deal meant that for the second time a key and very lucrative land sale by Haughey involved a company Traynor was a director of.

Robert Willis, a former director of CRH, told the inspectors about the origins of the company. 'I was managing director of Irish Life from 1967, and I think it was [in] about 1970 [that] a takeover bid was made by Roadstone Ltd for Irish Cement Ltd. Since Irish Life had a significant shareholding in each of those companies, a board was being formed and there was an awful lot of ruckus between the two companies. Irish Life was asked, or asked to have a representative on the board and I was asked to go on the board. That would have been around 1970 or whenever the merger took place.'

It was as a result of these developments that Willis got to know Traynor. 'I got to know him very well for a very long time, because the early days of Cement Roadstone were very torrid days. There was a lot of – I am sure I am talking in confidence here – but there was an awful lot of infighting. Unfortunately the two boards were just put together in mini-takeovers. The stronger eliminates the weaker. But the two came together and there was a great amount of argument, even physical argument, and if I may say, I got to know Traynor very well. He was a most sensible, calm, reasoned individual. I had a lot of time for him.' Seventeen years later, when Traynor was replacing Michael Dargan in the position of CRH chairman, Willis was still on the board and was involved in the process of Traynor's appointment.

Jim Culliton, another former director of CRH, also told the

inspectors about the company's early days. 'I joined Roadstone in 1952 as an 18-year-old... It was owned and managed to a large extent by Tom and Donal Roche... I found it a fantastic learning experience and it just grew and grew with the Irish economy. By 1970, which was the year of the merger with [Irish] Cement, it had reached profits of about £1 million and it was a publicly-quoted company. We had no intention of bidding for the cement company but they went on strike for five months and we had no raw materials and we would have ended up in serious financial difficulties, so we made what was regarded as an outrageous bid for Cement and we were satisfied at least that it would settle the strike very quickly, which it did in a couple of weeks.

'When the Cement Roadstone merger was formed, that was the first time I met Mr Traynor and that would have been in early 1971. He was in an usually powerful position even then because he was defending Cement against Roadstone. As managing director of Guinness Mahon he was the financial advisor. The merger would not have happened except that the British company, Readymix, bid for Roadstone in the middle of our bidding for [Irish] Cement, so we were seeking a merger with [Irish] Cement, and we were fighting off an unwelcome bid from the giant, Readymix. The government then took a hand because they did not want to see Roadstone getting into foreign hands, you could think like that in those days and they leaned on Irish Life who had about a 10 per cent shareholding in each company, to bring the two companies together.

'That is what happened, and we were fortunate that Seán Lemass, who had retired as Taoiseach, agreed to become independent chairman of the new company. Unfortunately, some months after he became chairman he fell into serious bad health and he died a year later. Unfortunately, we were then left without a chairman and serious rowing took place between Tom Roche and Ankerlund on the other, they being joint managing directors of the merged company. Lots of things happened that should not have happened and eventually after Bob Willis was chairman for a short time and had a holding operation, Michael Dargan was head hunted in as non-executive chairman.'

Jim Culliton was appointed chief executive of the merged company in 1974, following a competition. With the appointment came a position on the board. He began to work closely with Traynor. 'He was managing director of G&M and I was determined to make CRH into an international company. At the time, CRH was 95 per cent Republic of Ireland and we were extremely vulnerable because the economy had its good days and its bad days and we just came in and out with the tide.' Culliton would meet Traynor about three or four times a month to brief him on developments and plans. He met the other directors regularly as well, for the same reason. 'I formed a very high opinion of Des Traynor based on his performance in CRH.'

Anthony Barry, a civil engineer from Cork and brother of the former Fine Gael Minister for Foreign Affairs, Peter Barry, became a senior executive with CRH after the Cork firm he'd worked for, John A Wood, became part of CRH. In January 1988 he was appointed chief executive and from then on worked closely with Traynor. Barry told the inspectors that it was normal for a chairman who is required to be available at all times to a major company, to be provided with secretarial services which he could use for other business interests he might have. He said that at the time of Traynor's appointment he knew that Traynor had left G&M, but was still linked to the Cayman bank. 'I was generally aware that he had a continuing interest in banking.' Patrick Molloy, chairman of CRH at the time of the inspectors' inquiry, told them that, based on his inquiries, he believed that it was known at board level that Traynor had an ongoing interest in 'G&M/Ansbacher'.

The operation of the Ansbacher Deposits became a bit more complicated once Traynor had relocated to Fitzwilliam Square. Collery was still working for G&M down on College Green. In time, the money on deposit in G&M was moved to Irish Intercontinental Bank on Merrion Square, just down from Government Buildings. Letters and memos went from the CRH building in Fitzwilliam Square to the IIB building on Merrion Square. Because IIB did not have an over-the-counter cash service, Traynor opened an account with Bank of Ireland, St Stephen's Green, in the name of Kentford Securities. To get cash he would lodge an IIB draft drawn on the Ansbacher accounts to the Kentford account and withdraw cash. Sometimes the cash withdrawals were brought straight from the Bank of Ireland branch to the person making the withdrawal from their Ansbacher account, and sometimes the cash was brought back to the CRH offices for later collection. On other occasions bundles of cash were given to Traynor and he would bring them back to the CRH offices before sending them on for lodgement.

Traynor and Williams ran a busy office on Fitzwilliam Square. Cash and drafts came and went. Letters, faxes and phone calls to and from the Cayman Islands, most involving Furze, were a daily occurrence. It was a secret unauthorised bank working in the middle of the city, designed for the avoidance, if not the evasion, of tax. The Taoiseach was one of its customers, and the others included some of the top business figures of the day. Traynor walked around the city collecting drafts and cash from his customers, slipping them bits of paper showing them their balances, whispering to them that everything was in order, and that nothing was any problem.

Joan Williams, who gave evidence to the inspectors and to the Moriarty Tribunal, was a key figure in all of this. As well as helping Traynor run the Ansbacher operation she was herself a depositor. She said that it was Furze who opened her account for her, in the late 1970s or early 1980s. Furze used to come to Dublin regularly and set himself up in the G&M offices to work on balancing the books. 'It was on one occasion when he had been over here in Dublin working and he was staying at what is now Jurys Hotel. I don't know when it changed from Intercontinental to Jurys but Mr Traynor and Mr Furze and myself had been working a bit late in the office and Mr Traynor obviously had some sort of appointment and he asked me if I would give Mr Furze a lift back to his hotel. When I went up to get my car from the laneway where it was parked... fairly near the office... my car had been broken into, so we had to clear out the glass and everything before I could give Mr Furze a lift back.

'I think really he just felt sorry for me and sort of felt I might...

Instead of giving me a gift, which was what he usually did when he was leaving, he said he was going to open an account for me and put money into it.' Furze said she might like to save for a car. The following Christmas she received a fax from Furze telling her he had opened an account for her and placed some money in it as a Christmas present. The present may have been the second lodge-ment to the account. Williams was vague about the details. She said she did not receive regular statements on the account though she might have seen the balances from time to time. She said that when the Ansbacher statements were being prepared, Traynor would tear the top off them and then hand them to her, telling her who each one should be sent to. 'He might have said, "I see your balance is doing alright", or something like that. Or he might have shown me a piece of paper with it on it.' Her account was coded A/A7.

At some stage Williams began to receive payments of £250 sterling per month. These were lodged to her account. Records showing the payments being lodged, from 1992 on, were discovered by the inspec-tors. Williams said that Furze told her he was going to start lodging money to her account on a regular basis. Collery left G&M in 1989 and Williams, who was being paid by CRH at this stage, had to take on more duties in relation to the Dublin operations of the Cayman bank. Around the same time, Ansbacher had begun to move the deposits to Irish Intercontinental Bank. It seems that this was when Williams started to receive a payment every month. She told the inspectors that it was never explained to her that the payment was a fee.

Asked whether there was more work for her after Collery left G&M, she said that there possibly was. 'There was certainly more letters and that sort of thing because when we were dealing with Irish Intercontinental Bank everything was done by way of letter, whereas previously Mr Traynor probably would have phoned Mr Collery and asked him to do things through Guinness & Mahon or whatever, whereas when he wasn't available to do that obviously everything had to be done by letter to Irish Intercontinental Bank.' Williams said she did whatever Traynor asked her to do. 'If he asked me to type a letter about New Ireland or Aer Lingus equally I would have done it.'

Williams rarely withdrew money from the account. 'I tended to just leave it, the money, there, I sort of knew it was there in the background but I didn't really look on it as mine.' In 1996, she withdrew £9,152 sterling to buy a car. Traynor was dead by then, so she asked Collery for the money.

Occasionally, lodgements of £2,000 or £5,000 sterling were made to her account. Williams told the inspectors that she had no recollection of these lodgements. She said that Furze would occasionally say he was going to give her a 'gift'. In April 1995, a lodgement of £25,000 sterling was made. Williams said that this was when she ceased her work for Ansbacher and was told by Furze that a 'sort of farewell gratuity' was being paid to her.

Asked if she had ever declared the interest on the account to the Revenue, Williams said no. 'I never looked on this money as specifically mine. Maybe that sounds stupid or silly but I looked on it as just something that was there... in the background, if you like, if I needed it and my understanding, rightly or wrongly, was that it was only if I went to bring the money to Ireland that then I would obviously have to talk to the Revenue Commissioners.' Documents included in the Ansbacher Report show that the balance in account A/A7 in March 1996 was £82,112 sterling. Williams told the inspectors that she had no idea of the present state of her account. She had not been in contact with Collery or anyone else about it.

Collery, in his evidence, had an explanation for the regular payments Williams was receiving. Collery started his career with Lloyds bank in London in 1968, moved to G&M in 1974 and left G&M in 1989. From 1974 to the mid- or late 1990s Collery maintained the secret memorandum accounts. While he was with G&M, Collery was not paid over and above his G&M salary for his labours until 1986, the year Traynor left G&M. He told the inspectors: 'I seem to recall that it was at the suggestion of Mr Traynor that I should receive some remuneration for the services that I was giving to him and that he would arrange for funds to be put into an account in the bureau system.'

When Collery left G&M, the memorandum accounts on the bureau system were closed and moved to a computer which was installed in

Traynor's offices on Fitzwilliam Square. The related files were moved to the same location. Collery continued to maintain the accounts.

Collery's memorandum account was coded A/A30 and his initial payment was £1,250 sterling per month. The account was opened in January 1986 with an opening balance of £3,677.40 sterling. Two lodgements were made that month, one for £1,000 sterling and one for £125 sterling. The larger payment was for his work for Ansbacher, the smaller for his work for College Trustees and, later, a Cayman Islands company called Hamilton Ross Company Ltd. He said that he did not open a trust as his 'few shillings' did not warrant such a move. The work on the memorandum accounts was done during his normal working hours, late in the evenings and sometimes on Saturday mornings. When Collery moved from G&M and the memorandum account records were moved to Traynor's CRH offices, Collery continued to do the work but had to do it all on Saturday mornings. He would let himself into the CRH premises even though he had no link with the company whatsoever.

When he wanted to make a withdrawal from his account he would inform Traynor. The amounts were usually small. 'He would arrange for that cash to be available to me on the following, say, Saturday and left in my folder (in the CRH offices) to collect.' Sometimes, when Traynor was on holiday, Collery would be contacted by Williams to be told of people who wanted to make a withdrawal from their accounts, and he would organise it. Traynor had delegated the authority to Collery, to be used when Traynor was not available. This was the case from the early 1990s.

Collery got £1,000 sterling per month from Ansbacher between 1986 and 1989/1990, but the amount was then reduced to £750 sterling. This was because, he said, his new job did not leave him the time to be available for Traynor to the extent that he used to be. The amount paid was reduced accordingly. Collery thought that the bank continued to pay £1,000 sterling per month, but that from around this time Williams started to get £250 sterling of it, and he the rest. 'Miss Williams was going to do the additional work', so his fees were reduced.

In 1991 he was given two lump sum payments, £5,450 sterling and £6,875 sterling, which he said Traynor told him were 'gratuity for the service I had given him in the past'. Also around that time he would receive an occasional extra £1,000 sterling payment which was lodged to his account, and which he thought might have been for work done for particular clients in relation to the movement of their affairs from G&M to IIB. In 1995 he got a lump-sum payment of £5,000. He did not declare these payments to the Revenue.

As well as Williams and Collery, Traynor made use of two other people for the running of his clandestine banking activities. These were the caretaker of the CRH building on Fitzwilliam Square, and his CRH driver. Both were simply carrying out their duties as CRH employees, taking instructions from the company chairman. The CRH offices became the *de facto* Dublin branch office of the Cayman bank, and many of the 'normal' activities which would be carried out on a bank's premises began to occur in the chairman's office of the country's largest and most successful manufacturing company. Everything was done in full view of the CRH employees and executives who worked in or visited the building. It was a classic case of hiding in full view.

Number 42 Fitzwilliam Square was a regular Georgian terraced building. The front door worked on a buzzer which could be opened by a number of people in various parts of the building. The receptionist and the caretaker's room were on the ground floor and the chairman's office on the first floor. Beside Traynor's office was that of Williams, and on the same floor were the offices of the CRH company secretary. On the floors above Traynor's office there was a boardroom, the CRH secretarial department, the registry office and the insurance departments.

The caretaker would arrive at the offices at around 7.45 am each morning. Most days he was the first person to arrive, and most days Traynor was the first person to arrive after him. The post would arrive between 9 am and 10 am and the caretaker would sort it and leave it lying in bundles on a table in the hall. Envelopes addressed to G&M or Ansbacher were left on the table along with the other mail. They could be seen by anyone passing or anyone collecting the mail for themselves or their particular office.

Bank statements for the Ansbacher clients were prepared in the building. The computer which kept the data on the memorandum accounts was kept in Traynor's office and he would print out the statements. Each would have a heading on it identifying it as being a statement from Ansbacher or Hamilton Ross, and a code identifying the particular account and account holder. Traynor would use a ruler to tear off the top of the statement containing the Ansbacher or Hamilton Ross name, and the code, before passing on these headless statements to Williams. As each one was handed over he would tell Williams who to send it to. It was a laborious, time consuming job for a businessman of Traynor's importance.

Williams devised a system whereby she attached a loose piece of paper to each headless statement, so as to ensure she sent them to the proper owners. A mistake could be both embarrassing and disconcerting to a depositor. When putting the statements into the addressed envelopes, Williams would remove the slip of paper with the account holder's name on it and put in a compliments slip from Traynor. The statements were then sent out in the CRH post. This happened every quarter.

People called to Traynor's office and gave him cheques which they wanted to lodge to their accounts. He would pass them over to Williams with the necessary details and she would send them to G&M or, later, to IIB. Lodgements to G&M would be sent with a simple compliments slip and a handwritten note giving the instructions as to where to lodge the instrument. When the business was moved to IIB, more formal typed letters were used. Usually, these cheques or drafts were delivered to the bank by the caretaker, or by Traynor's CRH driver.

If someone wanted a cheque or draft drawn on their Ansbacher money, they would inform Traynor, who would in turn give Williams the necessary details. She would draft a letter to G&M or IIB and this would be delivered by the caretaker or driver. A copy of the letter would be put aside in Collery's file so that he could later make the necessary entry in the memorandum accounts. When G&M or IIB had the cheque or draft ready, a bank official would telephone Williams, and the caretaker or driver would be sent to the bank to collect the envelope which would be waiting in reception. This was happening on an ongoing regular basis. Each time the caretaker or driver found himself in G&M or IIB, he would check whether there was something waiting to be brought to 42 Fitzwilliam Square. In this way, many of the top business figures of the time made secret withdrawals from their clandestine, supposedly offshore accounts.

David Doyle, the son of P V Doyle, gave evidence to the Moriarty Tribunal about his offshore account and his dealings with Traynor. Traynor would dine in the Berkeley Court or Jurys Hotel most days of the week. The two hotels are in Ballsbridge and not far from Fitzwilliam Square. Traynor could be driven there in a matter of minutes, and he would usually arrive early for his appointment with whoever he was meeting that day. Traynor would stand in the lobby of the hotel so that he could greet his luncheon guest or guests upon their arrival. Doyle, if he had drafts or cheques or even cash he wanted to deposit in his offshore account, would approach Traynor in the lobby of the Berkeley Court Hotel and hand him an envelope containing the lodgement. 'Do you mean you would just go up to him and say, Mr Traynor, or Des, or however you addressed him, I want to give you some money for my account?' tribunal barrister, Jerry Healy SC, asked. Doyle replied: 'Yes.'

On one such occasion, in January 1987, a deposit of £27,000 was made in this way, including £2,000 in cash. Presumably, Traynor put the envelope away, had his lunch with whoever he was meeting that day, and brought the money back to his CRH offices afterwards. Doyle said that on other occasions he made his deposits by calling in at 42 Fitzwilliam Square.

Once, when he was making a withdrawal, he rang Traynor and told him how much he wanted. Traynor made an arrangement to see him in the hotel lobby a few days later, before lunch, and when he did he handed Doyle over a draft for the requested amount. This prompted the tribunal barrister to remark: 'There is no bank in

Ireland, England, or anywhere else for that matter, where the general manager or chief executive of the bank walks around and takes money from people at lunch parties or gives money to people at lunch parties or simply when he's passing through the doors of a hotel.' Doyle said that it didn't seem unusual at the time.

Withdrawals would be brought back to Traynor at 42 Fitzwilliam Square and he would then take them for passing on to his clients. He would have them delivered by the caretaker or his driver, or keep them on the premises for collection. When it was a cash withdrawal, Williams would always count the money at her desk to make sure the amount was correct. She would do this openly. She shared her office with another CRH employee and that secretary knew that the cash Williams was counting had nothing to do with CRH, but was rather to do with Traynor's non-CRH activities.

The driver and caretaker told the inspectors that they could remember regular cash withdrawals of between £1,000 and £8,000, although on occasion there were larger ones. The caretaker could recall a withdrawal of about £30,000, while the driver could remember a withdrawal he knew was much bigger than £8,000, because of the size of the box in which the money was contained. On that occasion, both Williams and the staff at G&M told him to take particular care. In December 1987, when Haughey was enjoying his first Christmas back in the office of Taoiseach after a few years sitting on the opposition benches, £57,000 in cash was withdrawn from his Ansbacher account and collected from G&M. It is not known if this is the withdrawal which stuck in the CRH driver's memory. Nor is it known if the driver or caretaker collected cheques or cash which were delivered to Haughey at Government Buildings.

Pádraig Collery would go to 42 Fitzwilliam Square to work on the computer in Traynor's office. This usually happened after office hours, or on Saturdays, and Collery, though he had no connection with CRH, had a key to the building. Staff knew he was to be allowed in and up to Traynor's office, and some of them knew him to see. They did not, of course, know what he was up to. A folder would be left for him containing copies of the letters or notes sent by

Williams during the proceeding period, and Collery would enter the deposits and withdrawals made from the various memorandum accounts. Up-to-date balances were produced on a monthly basis.

John Furze, during his regular visits to Dublin, would also visit the CRH offices in the way he used to visit the G&M offices. He would bring documentation with him and ensure that the Dublin records were in tune with those being kept in Cayman. He met GMCT clients in the CRH offices to discuss their affairs. CRH staff in the building knew Furze to see and knew that he was in the building in relation to the Cayman bank he helped run, and which Traynor was involved in, and which had letters sent to the CRH offices.

The driver and caretaker were never asked to keep quiet about the things they were being asked to do. The staff in Fitzwilliam Square, G&M and IIB all knew something of the correspondence and dealings involving a Cayman bank which were going on between Traynor and the Dublin banks. It seems that at least some senior members of the business community, who were not depositors, knew that Traynor could be contacted at the CRH offices in relation to banking and clients' money. When Ray McLoughlin of the public company, James Crean, was considering a rights issue, he and his advisers learned that it might be an idea to discuss it with Traynor, and that his, Traynor's, clients might be interested. McLoughlin met Traynor to discuss the matter in the CRH offices on Fitzwilliam Square.

Old pals: Des Traynor and Charles Haughey

Joan Williams, long-time secretary to Des Traynor, leaving the Moriarty Tribunal

John Mulhern, businessman and husband of Eimear Haughey, in his office in 1988

Cork businessman, Joseph Clayton Love Jr, behind Charles Haughey in April 1988

Jim Culliton addressing shareholders at the CRH Annual General Meeting in May 1974. Tom Roche is beside him, and Michael Dargan is next to Roche.

The Cement Roadstone building on Fitzwilliam Square, Dublin, where Des Traynor kept the Ansbacher files in the late 1980s and early 1990s.

Beef baron, Seamus Purcell, leaving the Moriarty Tribunal

Former Guinness & Mahon banker, Pádraig Collery, leaving the Moriarty Tribunal

Mary Harney, the leader of the Progressive Democrats, who sought the appointment of the Ansbacher inspectors.

Sam Field-Corbett, a long-time associate of Des Traynor, after he was questioned about the Ansbacher Deposits at the Moriarty Tribunal

Accountant and close friend of Des Traynor, Jack Stakelum

14

Members of the Board

Anumber of the most senior figures in CRH also became depositors. Tony Barry became chief executive of CRH in January 1988, and after his appointment began to work more closely with Traynor. Barry would regularly call into 42 Fitzwilliam Square early in the morning, at around 8 am, and go over a list of matters with Traynor concerning CRH. During one of these early-morning meetings, and after the two men had come to know each other, Barry mentioned a difficulty he had concerning the transfer of money to his children. Barry had some dividends coming to him from outside Ireland, mostly from investments in UK companies, and was also in receipt of some vouched CRH expenses being paid in sterling.

At the time, he had three children working abroad to whom he wanted to transfer money, as well as a daughter who was making preparations for marriage. Barry was unhappy about the exchange costs involved in converting his sterling money into Irish money and then sending the Irish money abroad. Every exchange led to a loss. Barry told the inspectors that Traynor had said to him: 'Well, there are simple ways over that which are quite in order. I can set them up for you. I still have banking connections and all you do is transfer the money to me and I will keep an account and so long as it is strictly for your children, you tell me when you want it transferred and I will transfer it.' The matter was discussed a number of times and by early

1989 Barry took up the offer. The account was opened without Barry signing any documentation.

Barry was regularly out of the country on CRH business, often for weeks at a time, and it was during these trips that he would incur expenses. When he returned he would submit for the expenditure incurred and be reimbursed with a sterling cheque. CRH had a company in the Channel Islands called Bluehill Investments which was used for tax and finance planning in relation to CRH's interests outside Ireland. The company was set up with the permission of the Central Bank and operated under the regulation of the Central Bank. Sam Field-Corbett was involved in the running of Bluehill and was authorised to sign its cheques. Field-Corbett's company, Management Investment Services, handled the payroll for the senior executives of CRH. The Bluehill cheques Barry would get might be for thousands of pounds. 'I would get a cheque, put it in an envelope, send it to him (Traynor) and say, please credit to my account.' He would send on sterling dividend cheques in a similar matter. Mostly, these cheques were sent to Traynor in the internal CRH post.

Barry said that he subsequently learned that Traynor owned part of GMCT and had sold it to the Ansbacher group, but he couldn't recall when he learned this. He knew his account was in the Cayman Islands. He got bank statements from Traynor but the tops of the statements, which contained the name of the bank, had been torn off.

While the money Barry put in his account was not money he was hiding from the Revenue, he did not declare the interest he was earning on the account. The amount of tax due on the interest would have been very small in the context of his overall earnings.

Jim Culliton, who joined the board of CRH in 1974 when he was appointed to the position of chief executive, was asked by the inspectors how he came to have a Cayman account. 'I clearly remember him (Traynor) suggesting the facility to me. May I say I take full responsibility for my own mistakes in this, but if you bear in mind that he was a very senior director of CRH, he was on the remuneration committee and he was on the finance committee. More than that he was representing the Cement side of the house, which was sort of two-thirds [Irish] Cement and one-third Roadstone, they being the relative sizes of the two companies. I may have provoked his offer to me in that I probably was referring to the very high tax rates at the time, the top rates of tax in the 1970s were 70 per cent to 77 per cent. I did not initiate it. I did not know about it.'

Traynor told Culliton that he could open a demand account for him. Culliton had £10,000 to £12,000 in a domestic bank account, and he transferred it into the account Traynor had offered to open for him. 'It was quite clear to me that it was to be secret. I got no application form to sign, no documents, no statements and there was no reference to fees or commissions for Guinness & Mahon or Des Traynor.' Culliton's account was opened in 1979 and he did not declare the interest earned on the account to the Revenue. He told the inspectors he believed the money was going to be placed on deposit in the Channel Islands. 'I had never heard of the Cayman Islands twenty years ago,' he said. He assumed it was the Channel Islands 'because at that time that is where offshore funds went.'

'From time-to-time I gave Des Traynor money to put in. From time-to-time I visited him in Trinity Street. He had an office just at the back of Guinness & Mahon and I would have been in and out anyway to brief him between board meetings on CRH affairs. If I needed money I only needed to give him a few days notice or if I had money to put in, I could bring it in and give it to him in the bank. All my dealings with him until I closed the account were in Trinity Street in his bank.' The drawings were almost always in cash.

Culliton retired in 1986. 'It was entirely my own decision. I had been 13 years as chief executive, which is a very long time. The company was transformed and we had huge interests in America and mainland Europe and so on.' The value of the company had grown from £25 million when he took up the position of chief executive, to £700 million when he retired. 'At the same time Michael Dargan had decided to step down as chairman, he having been about 14 years in the chair and Des Traynor was chosen unanimously by the board to become chairman at the AGM in May 1987.'

Tony Barry was chief executive designate, and Culliton decided that there was no point in his forming a relationship with Traynor if he was to be replaced a few months after Traynor's appointment. He told Traynor and Barry to start to get to know each other 'because the relationship between a chairman and a chief executive was hugely important in a big group, the chemistry has to be right.'

Because of the huge contribution Culliton had made to the success of CRH, Traynor thought that he should be given a large golden handshake by the company. However, a direct payment to Culliton could have a significant knock-on effect on the cost of his pension, as the pension was based on his final year remuneration from CRH. 'Another reason I think why he didn't want it to be seen in the annual report to have made a big £100,000 or £120,000 payment was that Mr Haughey had become Taoiseach in August 1987 and had brought in a sort of hair-shirt environment where everything was frozen and there were cutbacks in health services and so on. Wages and directors fees and all that sort of thing were being watched very carefully.'

The money for Culliton was organised by Traynor from an off-shore CRH company, and in such a way that the details did not end up in the company's annual report. It seems the money was given to Culliton in instalments, and that it was given to him by Traynor, sometimes in cash. 'It was CRH's money coming backwards and there was no tax advantage because it was explained to me that these were gifts that were perfectly in order.'

Culliton wanted to close his account when he was retiring from his executive role in CRH, and closed the account in mid-1987. Eleven years later, in 1998, (after the deposits had been discovered) he calculated as best he could the interest he had earned on the account over the years, the tax which should have been paid, and the interest and penalties he might owe as a result of not paying that tax. He calculated the entire amount to be £26,000. Because he wanted to be sure he'd dealt with the matter, he paid £50,000. He paid the money anonymously, through a solicitor. 'The reason I did it on an anonymous basis was I just did not want to create more trouble for my own company, CRH, and Des Traynor.'

Of Traynor, he told the inspectors: 'I am bewildered by the revelations about Des Traynor... because that is not the man that I knew
as a colleague, I have to say that. I really am bewildered, he just
fooled us all.' Culliton thought Traynor had left G&M to take on the
role of chairman of CRH and didn't know that Traynor had had a
falling-out with G&M, and that there had been some issue between
Traynor and the bank concerning a bad loan. 'I didn't know anything
about that, nor did we when we came to select a chairman. He is a
complete enigma. He was a very able and likeable person. There was
nothing cold or calculating about Des Traynor. He was a most com-
passionate man and I am as bewildered as many people reading about
the events of the last while, having been close to him.'

Michael Dargan gave evidence on oath to the inspectors but the
transcript did not appear in the appendices to the Ansbacher Report.
Why this is so is not clear. Dargan was a very successful civil servant
and businessman who served as chairman of both CRH and Aer
Lingus, and was a member of the board of the Bank of Ireland.
According to the report, Dargan told the inspectors that his memory
was unreliable. He said he had no recollection of having any funds
in Ansbacher. Nevertheless, the inspectors named him as an
Ansbacher client.

'Documentary evidence indicates that a guarantee given by
Guinness & Mahon for a loan obtained from a Brussels bank by Dr
Dargan in 1990, was backed by an Ansbacher deposit. There is also
documentary evidence of a transfer of funds from an Ansbacher
account in IIB to accounts in Dr Dargan's name in Ulster Bank and
Bank of Ireland.' Dargan's solicitor, on his behalf, strongly objected
to any finding that Dargan might have been a client of Ansbacher.

Dargan gave evidence to the Moriarty Tribunal. The tribunal,
when examining the affairs of Celtic Helicopters, found that a cheque
for £10,000, made out to Dargan, had been lodged to an Amiens
account in G&M to form part of the start-up capital of Ciarán
Haughey's helicopter company. Dargan insisted that he never gave
any contribution towards the company. He said he was involved in

some stud farm dealings with his son, who lived abroad, and would use Traynor when sending money abroad to him. Amazingly, given that he was on the board of the Bank of Ireland from the mid-1970s to the late 1980s, Dargan said he had not been aware of the exchange control regulations which governed the transfer abroad of funds at the time.

The £10,000 cheque was not the only one of Dargan's to be found in the Amiens account. Another five cheques made out to him were similarly lodged. It is possible that the cheques were lodged to the account as part of a switching operation, with the Irish money being used in Ireland, while the sterling or dollar equivalent was transferred from a GMCT client's account, or clients' accounts, on to Dargan's son.

Gerald Hickey was a solicitor and businessman who was an active supporter of Fianna Fáil and a member of Taca. He was on the boards of CRH and New Ireland Assurance, companies of which Des Traynor was chairman, acted as a solicitor to G&M, and was involved in a number of property developments where funds were borrowed from G&M. He was chairman of the Hickey Beauchamp O'Reilly legal firm. His dealings with Ansbacher would seem to have had little to do with CRH.

Hickey first met Traynor in the late 1960s. Both Hickey and Traynor were appointed to the board of New Ireland Assurance in 1971 and came to know one another well. They also knew each other because Hickey had dealings with G&M, borrowing money for property speculation. At the time, interest on borrowings was deductible against income tax and a lot of professionals were taking out loans which they then used for speculative purposes. The cost of servicing the loans was subsidised, so to speak, by the income tax savings. The net effect was that instead of paying income tax you could speculate on shares or property or other investments. He was also involved in the creation of CRH out of Roadstone and Irish Cement. Traynor saw Hickey in action as solicitor for New Ireland Assurance and asked him to do work for G&M, which Traynor was running at the time.

Hickey told the inspectors that he was involved with a company called Clonmel Estates which bought property at the bottom of Abbey Street in Dublin, opposite the VHI headquarters. Conditions were not right for development and the company held on to the site hoping something would happen, and something did. Irish Life decided it was going to build a large, new office complex and wanted to buy the site from Clonmel Estates. The deal was done, Clonmel Estates made a profit of about £210,000, and was afterwards left with nothing but this money on deposit. Hickey said that he liquidated the company and distributed the cash. Tax should have been paid on the distribution, but was not.

Hickey said that he had a one-third interest in Clonmel Estates. Asked who else was involved, he mentioned two foreigners who were not resident in Ireland, and whom he did not want to name as he acted as a solicitor for them in relation to the matter. He said that their names did not appear in any of the Clonmel Estates documents as they were 'sleeping partners'. Hickey said he placed his third from the deal on deposit with G&M by giving a cheque to Traynor. The cheque was for £211,000, the entire profits from the Clonmel deal (which G&M had been involved in financing). Hickey's share was £70,214.29. He told the inspectors he asked the bank to put his money in a short-term deposit account as he would need the money for another deal he had planned for about a year later. He said that he had assumed that the bank would put the money on deposit in Ireland. He also said that he did not know what happened to the other two shares, even though he was acting on their behalf in relation to Clonmel Estates.

Hickey said Traynor knew about the matter. Asked how, he said: 'He knew about everything that went on.' Hickey said that Traynor was not one of the sleeping partners involved in the deal, although Traynor was party to other deals which Hickey was involved in. Hickey said that he did not believe that G&M knew who his two 'sleeping partners' were in the Clonmel Estates deal. He said that initially G&M put the entire £211,000 on deposit in his name 'because they didn't know who the other people were.'

Hickey said that he continued to act as solicitor for the two foreigners. He would get statements on their deposits 'if they were required at all. These people didn't take any notice of the thing for years.' When they did contact him, he contacted G&M and got the latest balance and relayed it back to his clients. 'They didn't come near me for years.' Hickey said that he knew that the other two-thirds was on deposit in the Cayman Islands, and that his was as well. He said that he withdrew his third in 1980 for another speculative deal, involving the Dolphin Hotel. A company he had set up bought the Dolphin Hotel, in East Essex Street, Dublin, in the 1970s. It had proven difficult to develop, and for a few years the only use it was put to was to operate as a pub.

Hickey said that he had been given an 'indication' that the State might be interested in the building as a courthouse. 'That is the only reason I took a chance on the development. I was wrong because the price of the building went bananas in the course of the construction.' The venture did not produce a profit. ICC, which had put money into the venture, took a hit. Hickey was on the board of the bank at the time. 'It was extremely embarrassing,' he told the inspectors. The building is now a courthouse.

Hickey was asked about the two partners in the Clonmel Estates deal. He said that they were from continental Europe. Pressed to reveal their identity he said he had a difficulty with that because of the rules on solicitor-client confidentiality. He said that he had taken advice on the matter, and the advice was not to disclose the identities. He said that they were two people, husband and wife, and that the husband was dead, and he wasn't sure where the wife was.

One of the inspectors, Noreen Mackey, put it to Hickey that there was nothing on paper to indicate anything other than that he was the sole owner of Clonmel Estates. He said that a 'gentleman's agreement' lay behind the formal legal arrangement that appeared on the documentation.

Hickey said that he found Traynor to be very astute. 'He had many ways of concealment other than numbered or lettered accounts.' He said that Traynor would tell him to buy property in the name of shelf companies. He would not know who was behind them. Traynor might have been. Hickey would buy the property, as a solicitor, for the unknown purchaser. The money was always paid on time. 'Then, in due course, I would sell the property and I would send the proceeds, of course, back to G&M.' He did not expand on this, but seemed to be indicating that Traynor would 'conceal' money in property deals.

He said that Traynor had a photographic memory. 'He knew every transaction that was going on.' He would sometimes put accountants or solicitors names on documents so that if he did forget a detail, he would know who to contact. G&M always paid 'on the dot. They were the best payers ever.' He had a great deal of confidence in G&M and in Traynor. 'People gave him millions, as you know. Everybody had complete confidence in him. He was regarded as a totally honest man and also as a totally able man.'

Hickey took out borrowings over the years which were described in G&M documentation as being suitably secured, the phrase used by the bank to indicate that offshore deposits were being used as backing security. A document, dated April 1978, shows such a loan to the value of £211,018, a similar amount to the profit from the Clonmel Estates deal. Hickey said that it was suggested to him by Traynor and Don Reid, of Stokes Kennedy Crowley, that he set up a discretionary trust, but he never did. He sat in on meetings where Traynor discussed offshore trusts with G&M clients.

Hickey was in poor health in May 2000 when he gave evidence to the inspectors. He was interviewed privately by the Moriarty Tribunal about his dealings with Ansbacher. He died before the inspectors' report was published. In their report, the inspectors said that subsequent to his being interviewed by them, Hickey had withdrawn his claim that two others had been involved with him in the Abbey Street deal. It seems that the two foreigners, whom Hickey had refused to identify for reasons of legal privilege, were a fiction.

Another CRH director who had dealings with Traynor and Ansbacher, Diarmuid Quirke, died in September 1994. He had been an executive director of CRH from 1980 until his retirement in

1991. It seems that Quirke, like Tony Barry, incurred expenses while travelling abroad for CRH, and was reimbursed by Bluehill, the CRH company based in Guernsey. A note found by the inspectors, dated January 1992, read: 'I enclose second statement for sterling expenses for calendar year 1991. I would request that you would forward your cheque to Ms Joan Williams at 42 Fitzwilliam Square who will be authorised to deal with it on my behalf.' Cheques from Bluehill, and payable to Quirke, were lodged to the Ansbacher account in IIB. In January 1992, $4,000 was withdrawn from the Ansbacher account in G&M and used to buy traveller's cheques for Quirke and his wife. In September 1993 a further £1,324 is known to have been withdrawn in a similar way. It is not known when the account was closed. Quirke's wife told the inspectors she'd known nothing about any Ansbacher account.

Robert Willis, the man from Irish Life who joined the CRH board, also opened an Ansbacher account, and again it was so that he could lodge payments from CRH to it. He was on a board committee which, some time in the late 1970s, began to generate fees for him and which also led to him incurring expenses which he recouped from CRH. 'The fees would have gone through the PAYE system. The expense allowances were paid gross. I gave those cheques to my business colleague, Des Traynor, as whatever he was, managing director of Guinness & Mahon Ireland, to open a deposit account. I was saving, I didn't, it was spare money, so far as I was concerned, and I opened a deposit account.' The account was opened in the early 1980s. 'It was convenient. I was getting the cheques from CRH and he was across the table or in the coffee room, or whatever, and I saw him a couple of times a month. Each amount of money was relatively small, a couple of thousand. I think they were paid half-yearly.' On occasion, he called into Traynor in G&M and handed him the cheques there.

At times, Willis would ask Traynor to transfer a few thousand to an account he had in London. 'I kept small balances in it, a couple of thousand, and when I was over there my wife shopped. It was personal.' He all but closed the GMCT account in 1987 and used the

approximately £70,000 he withdrew to help his son buy an apartment. In 1990, Traynor contacted him and told him there was still a
small sum in the account. Willis thinks he got the money from
Traynor, about £5,000.

At first Willis believed that he had an account with G&M in
Dublin. Traynor would give him slips of paper with his balance on it
and when Willis asked questions he didn't get answers. He got an
assurance from Traynor: 'You have nothing to worry about, your
money is in Dublin, you have full access to it whenever you want.'

Willis said that from time to time he 'was handed in an envelope,
obviously by Des, a piece of paper, that would have shown my
balance and presumably any additions and interest. I think it had my
name. I knew it was mine, I know this sounds awfully naive but I
would totally trust Des Traynor. I sat with him for years.'

He would ask Traynor why the paper had no heading on it, and
would be told not to worry. 'As time went on, sure, I felt everything
wasn't quite kosher, but either I hadn't the guts or I didn't want to
ask or find out what he had done with my money. I was giving it to
him to put into an account in Dublin and that is what I believed.'

Willis said that the role of CRH chairman was a very demanding
one and that Traynor was very good at it. 'For all the things that he
has allegedly done, and indeed rather let me down, he was a very
good chairman and he was a busy one, he would have entertained, but
I presume it wasn't full time. I didn't sit in judgment on him. But lots
of things got done in CRH when he became chairman, including
renovating the board.'

He said that he was shocked when he read about what Traynor
had been up to in the CRH offices. He said that he had been aware
that Traynor had left G&M when he became chairman of CRH, but
he kept giving him the cheques. 'There seemed to be no problem, I
trusted the guy 100 per cent and I didn't have any difficulty.' He did
not know that Traynor was carrying on a *de facto* banking business
from the CRH offices. He said that the board never knew what was
going on. Traynor got no permission to use the premises in the way he
did. He wasn't sure if what Traynor did was in breach of his fiduciary

duty as a CRH director. 'I have to ask myself what is banking business. It wasn't a little man behind a grille taking in money. Speaking personally, I would not have expected CRH's chairman's office to be used for this sort of business.'

Richard Wood was a director of John A Wood Ltd, Cork, a company established by his father. Wood Sr and three friends were involved in property developments in Youghal, Cork City and Dublin – developments in which they made use of G&M. They also made use of Haughey Boland. In June 1969, Traynor, who was still with Haughey Boland, had dealings with John Furze, who was then with the Bank of Nova Scotia in the Cayman Islands, in relation to these developments. Offshore companies and trusts were established to receive the profits from the property development projects in Ireland. This is the earliest known contact between Furze and Traynor, and pre-dates Traynor's official move to G&M, and that bank's establishment of a company or bank in the Cayman Islands. Money was paid over in November 1969 for the establishment of these Cayman companies and trusts. When his father died in 1972, Richard Wood became involved in these property developments. Sam Field-Corbett provided secretarial services to some of the companies involved. The Crampton building group, which was a customer of G&M, was involved in some of the developments. George Crampton, the chairman and managing director of Cramptons, and five other Crampton directors, set up Cayman trusts in the early 1970s, having taken advice from Don Reid, and having been told by lawyers that what they were doing was legal. The funds lodged came from the development of the ACC Bank building on the corner of Hatch Street and Harcourt Street.

One development Wood was involved in was the conversion of Portobello House, Dublin, from a nursing home to offices. Another, Scotch House, involved people called Rhatigan. Mr Brian Rhatigan, of Rhatigan Holdings and Rhatigan Developments, was identified in the Ansbacher Report as a client of Ansbacher, but he denied any involvement with the Cayman bank.

John A Wood became part of CRH in the 1970s, and the Wood family received CRH shares as part of the deal. The CRH shares were used as backing for loans from G&M used in property development. Loans were also secretly backed by Cayman deposits.

Wood received statements from Furze in the Cayman Islands informing him as to what was on deposit there. He thought he received the statements about once every year. The Cayman accounts were closed in 1977, and the money, £78,374, repatriated to Ireland.

In a letter to the inspectors after his interview, Wood, having spoken to some former associates of his father, wrote: 'In the late Sixties my father made the decision to enter the property development business as a sideline. Taxation on such developments was so high and determined in such a harsh manner, all profit being treated as income in the year that it arose, and therefore subject to the highest rate, that businessmen attempted to find legitimate ways around this problem, which had the effect of stunting the development of Dublin and elsewhere, and hindering economic activity.

'In my father's case, he was advised to go to Messrs Haughey Boland for accounting and taxation advice and it was there that he first met Mr Des Traynor. Mr Traynor devised the scheme which was put in place, the details of which I have already given to you. Incidentally, this was some years before Mr Traynor and my father became colleagues on the board of Cement Roadstone Holdings Ltd (now CRH plc), which was created by the merger of [Irish] Cement Ltd and Roadstone Ltd. Mr Traynor had been on the board of [Irish] Cement Ltd, and my father had been on the board of Roadstone Ltd.' He said there was never any suspicion that Mr Traynor's scheme was illegal; neither his father or his father's colleagues would have countenanced such a thing.

Wood was a director of CRH from 1981 to 1997, and would meet Traynor at board meetings and on CRH trips to view new facilities. Wood said that he believed that the scheme involving the Cayman Islands and the property development companies was devised by Traynor. 'My understanding of it was that it was taking advantage of a loophole in the laws or a weakness in the laws and I was certainly not aware that there was anything illegal about it. Mr Traynor was, after all, a banker and those were the days when one trusted bankers. I would be very surprised, I don't think any of us felt that there was anything illegal about it.' He made the point that he was involved in selecting Traynor as Chairman of CRH in 1986/1987. 'Obviously we would not have selected anyone whom we felt had been involved in illegality. In the light of subsequent information that may seem rather extraordinary, but that certainly was the case at the time.'

Part Five

Things Fall Apart

15

Des Traynor Dies

Johm Desmond Traynor died in his sleep at home on 11 May 1994. He was 62 years old, married, with six children and nine grandchildren. 'It was very, very sudden,' Pádraig Collery told the inspectors. 'He was in the States, and indeed was planning to go back to the States later in the year because his son was getting married there, and it was coinciding with the World Cup in the States at that particular time and he was an avid soccer supporter, so [he] was looking forward very much to that. He had to come back from the States, had attended some board meeting, and called me on, I think, the Tuesday to say could I meet with him on that Saturday and I said, "of course", and then on that Wednesday morning he was found dead in his bed, so it was that sudden.'

His passing was noted in the newspapers and his funeral was attended by a large number of representatives of the upper reaches of Ireland's business community. Furze travelled from the Cayman Islands. Haughey attended the funeral and spoke about his friend. There were a number of discreet conversations during the funeral, not least one between Furze and Haughey. Haughey was told that Collery would now be the man to speak to in Dublin about his Ansbacher money. A number of people, it seems, were being given similar advice. Traynor operated in great secrecy and there was no system in place for dealing with his sudden departure. Many of his clients, according to their evidence to the inspectors, didn't know where their money was, or who to contact.

Traynor's death was noted in the *Irish Times*. In a twelve-paragraph report Traynor's connection with John Byrne and the involvement Traynor had had with the disgraced former premier of Western Australia, Brian Burke, were mentioned before the various posts and positions he held at the time of his death were listed. A few days later a letter from John Gore-Grimes was published, saying that the report 'grossly misrepresented the real character and talent of the late J D Traynor. To write off the achievements of this man in such a negative way does not reflect the many genuine contributions which Des made to the Irish business community.'

Gore-Grimes complained that the report had caused distress to Traynor's family and friends, and expressed the hope that a fair and balanced assessment might be published in the future. On the same page of the same edition an appreciation appeared, signed by JPC, who said that Traynor's non-existent public profile could be attributed to the fact that Traynor 'detested the cult of personality'. It was a strange line to be associated with someone who'd spent his life helping Haughey live like a lord on other people's money.

The appreciation continued: 'He had rare natural talents and his financial acumen and shrewd judgement were such that he was frequently consulted by the highest in the land. He had many fine qualities and was a good listener. He took everything in, and when he spoke you listened. Des was the person you went to if you were in trouble and he took great pride in helping you resolve your difficulties. His dry wit was legendary; one-liners were his speciality.'

Pádraig Collery and John Furze went around to the CRH offices on Fitzwilliam Square on the Saturday after the funeral. Collery used his key to let them in and the two men went up to the CRH chairman's office and unplugged the computer which had been used to maintain the memorandum accounts. They carried the computer down the stairs and brought it out and put it in the boot of their car. Then they went back up and collected two small filing cabinets containing Ansbacher documents, and brought those down to the car. Collery had asked Field-Corbett if he could use Field-Corbett's offices to store the computer and files and Field-Corbett had agreed. The offices were on Winetavern Street, the steep street that goes from Christ Church down towards the quays and the Four Courts. Field-Corbett's offices were on the left of the street as you descended, in one of a short terrace of low, new office buildings.

Collery had been allocated a corner of an office in the premises and set up the computer and the filing cabinets. When Furze left to return to the Cayman Islands he brought some of the GMCT files with him. Later in the year he returned to Dublin and destroyed many of the files which still remained there, and brought more back to the Cayman Islands with him. From now on the bulk of the work which was done from the Winetavern Street offices was to do with the smaller accounts kept in the name of Hamilton Ross. For a number of reasons, including Ansbacher's change of attitude towards the Dublin business, and people wanting to close down their Ansbacher business following Traynor's death, the Ansbacher, as opposed to the Hamilton Ross, end of things began to wind down. That said, some of the larger Ansbacher clients, such as John Byrne, continued to make use of Ansbacher and the services of IIB.

Collery had been given both the use of the office at Winetavern Street, and the partial use of some of Field-Corbett's staff. The type of letter which used to arrive at Traynor's CRH offices now began to arrive at Field-Corbett's offices. Telephone messages were taken by the staff for Collery and some clients collected money from their accounts by calling at the offices. Field-Corbett became a signatory of the Hamilton Ross accounts and signed letters on behalf of the company. Overall, Field-Corbett, who up to this had provided back-up services to many Ansbacher clients and served as a conduit to Traynor and the offshore funds, now became more involved. He was paid £35,000 sterling by Furze for this work and despite his attempts to play down the importance of his involvement, the inspectors decided he was, after Traynor's death, an agent of Hamilton Ross in Dublin.

He was also working for a number of Ansbacher clients. Ron Woss, the Australian who sat on the board of Danstar and Tepbrook, the two companies which formed part of John Byrne's trust structures, attended Traynor's funeral and met with Field-Corbett. After this, Corbett became more involved in the running of the account known as the Diamond Trust account, sending weekly faxes to Woss in Australia. Prior to Traynor's death, Field-Corbett had already been involved with this matter, though to a lesser extent. During his interview with the inspectors he said that he had little or no involvement with the account up to the time of Trayor's death. This prompted Judge O'Leary to comment: 'Mr Field-Corbett, you are not suffering from any disease which would impair your memory now, are you?' Field-Corbett replied: 'I don't know.'

By the time of Traynor's death there was no longer any link between G&M and the Cayman Islands. The Cayman bank had been bought by the Henry Ansbacher group and renamed Ansbacher Cayman Ltd. The Irish deposits were with Irish Intercontinental Bank. There were also deposits there in the name of Hamilton Ross Company Ltd, the Cayman company used for some smaller accounts and for people particulary close to Traynor.

Richard Fenhalls was a key figure in much of what happened in the years prior to Traynor's death. Fenhalls was appointed chief executive of the Guinness Mahon group, based in London, in 1981. He had formerly been a director of IIB. In 1984, when G&M had solvency problems because of disastrous venture capital investments which had produced a loss of £7 million, Fenhalls devised the plan whereby the Dublin bank sold its Cayman subsidiary to the London Guinness Mahon group. Shortly thereafter, Fenhalls quit the group and took up the position of chief executive of the Henry Ansbacher group.

In 1986, Traynor had a row with London and left G&M but continued as chairman of Guinness Mahon Cayman Trust. Fenhalls, in his new position as chief executive of Ansbacher, telephoned Traynor and told him that if GMCT ever became available, Ansbacher would be interested in buying it. By this time GMCT had US and Jamaican depositors as well as Irish ones. Some time in 1988, Traynor phoned Fenhalls and told him that he, Furze, Collins and Hugh Hart, a Jamaican national, were 'tired of what was going on in the Guinness Mahon group' and wanted to buy the Cayman bank for themselves. He said that once they had done so they might sell it to the Ansbacher group. Fenhalls wanted to deal directly with the Guinness Mahon group, but Traynor persuaded him not to for reasons which are unclear. The developments Traynor had outlined then came to pass. When Ansbacher bought the Cayman bank in August 1988, it paid Traynor and his colleagues £750,000 in cash, and shares in Ansbacher worth £2.25 million. There were a number of other associated share dealings, including Traynor and his colleagues buying Ansbacher/GMCT shares worth £750,000. This deal was for 75 per cent of GMCT. In time, the remainder of the shares in the Cayman bank were bought by the Ansbacher group, and the Cayman bank's name was changed to Ansbacher Cayman.

G&M was not doing at all well as a business in the mid- to late 1980s, making losses every two out of three years. The Cayman bank, in contrast, was making profits of about £750,000 per annum. By 1990 Fenhalls was worried about the credit worthiness of G&M and thought that it was not safe for his Cayman bank to have so much money on deposit with the Dublin bank. By 1987 the deposits in G&M had grown to £57 million. The Cayman bank was also making significant deposits in the London Guinness Mahon bank, and in 1987 the Cayman deposits in London were £81 million sterling. It was a lot of money to have in a bank you had concerns about.

Fenhalls discussed the matter with Traynor. He told the inspectors that Traynor was at first reluctant but eventually agreed to move the money to IIB. Fenhalls paved the way for the move, as he was well known in IIB, having formerly served as a director there. The transfer of the money was done over a period of two years, as the loss of such a large proportion of its deposits could have been a mortal blow to G&M if it had occurred suddenly.

When the deposits began their move to IIB, Traynor opened an account in the name of Kentford Securities with the Bank of Ireland in St Stephen's Green. This account was operated in a way similar to the Amiens accounts Traynor had in G&M, as a sort of staging post for money travelling in and out of the Cayman accounts. It also had another function. IIB had no cash facility and Traynor used the Kentford account to get around this problem. If a client wanted money in cash, Traynor would request a cheque from IIB drawn on the Ansbacher account, lodge it to Kentford, and then make a cash withdrawal. Large amounts of cash were withdrawn in this way.

Meanwhile, the Ansbacher group's auditors were getting a bit worried about what the Cayman bank they had bought was up to. The Cayman bank was known within the group as the 'Irish bank', even though many of its customers were now from the US and the Caribbean. It was run in what one banker described as an 'entrepreneurial' fashion, as against the more staid, conventional 'bankerly' fashion. Questions began to be asked about the relationship between the bank and its Irish customers, and specifically about the role Traynor was playing in Dublin. It seems that the complete picture of what was going on may not have been known to the Ansbacher group at the time it bought the Cayman bank. That seems a bit odd, but it is the impression given by the evidence gathered by the Ansbacher inspectors.

When questions were first raised about what Traynor was up to in Dublin, Fenhalls responded by defending the Irish whizz-kid: 'I find it inconceivable to make the assumption that the chairman of Ireland's largest company (CRH), director of a number of prestigious Irish companies, adviser to the great and good in Dublin and approved by the Central Bank of Ireland to be a fit and proper person to run a bank would be conducting improper, illegal and clandestine activities contrary to the law.' He suggested that Ansbacher people visit 'Des', work out how he operated, and report back to the group's audit committee.

Inquiries in Dublin met with reassurances as to the propriety of what was going on. Nevertheless, the unease persisted and within a year the whole matter had developed into something of a crisis. It seems that the Ansbacher people in London were initially happy with the Cayman bank, but quickly changed their minds and decided that they wanted Furze and Collins out of any executive function. There was a clash between the old owners and the new ones. In time, the view in relation to Furze and Collins was extended to Traynor. Much of the concern had to do with the 'Dublin accounts'.

Within a year, Fenhalls had changed his tune regarding Des Traynor. In September 1992 he wrote in an internal memo: 'With regard to Des Traynor, my view is that the sort of business he can usefully introduce to the Cayman Islands is more than out-weighed by the regulatory risks involved in his conducting a pseudo-banking business in Dublin.' This view was in relation to the overall Ansbacher business in Dublin. Fenhalls thought that he might ask Traynor to move it to a bank of Traynor's choice. Coincidentally, on the same day he wrote the note he also received a fax from the Cayman Islands which caused him further concern.

The fax was from an official from Ansbacher in London who had been appointed to the Cayman bank. It described how the Cayman company, Hamilton Ross, was being used in relation to the Dublin business. At this stage, Hamilton Ross was managed and nominally owned by Furze, and used the same address as Ansbacher Cayman. It was being used as a company which collected funds for onward transmission to Ansbacher, and itself had no reserves. About 250 transactions per month were being passed across the Hamilton Ross memorandum accounts maintained by Collery. The money deposited in Ireland was being received by Hamilton Ross and then banked in IIB on behalf of Ansbacher Cayman, i.e. in the name of Ansbacher. The problem from the Cayman bank's point of view was that money was being collected from people in Dublin and being lodged in Dublin in the name of Ansbacher Cayman, and the Cayman bank did not know who these people were and had no control over their affairs, other than that exercised by Traynor. If anything went wrong, the clients would be likely to blame Ansbacher.

The fax from the Cayman Islands pointed out a number of difficulties arising from what Traynor was up to. These were: deposit-taking in Ireland without a licence; trading without telling the Irish revenue; breaching exchange control regulations; assisting Irish residents to evade tax; failing to comply with money laundering regulations; the possibility of errors arising before the money was deposited with

Ansbacher; and the absence of the normal dual controls over what Traynor was doing.

It seems that Fenhalls was surprised when told about the Hamilton Ross accounts and felt that Traynor was involved in something which constituted a betrayal of his, Fenhalls', trust in him. It was decided that the Irish business would have to go, and that Traynor's position was 'untenable and he would have to go in due course.'

Traynor, when approached, assured Ansbacher that no laws were being broken. At some stage, Fenhalls sought assurance from Traynor that none of the clients he was acting for in Dublin were involved in money laundering or drugs or anything of that nature. Traynor assured him that he knew all his clients and that there was no question of any such activity. This was true, of course, in relation to the Dublin clients, though as we have seen, Furze had involved Dublin in dealings with the Pruna drugs traffickers and their associates.

Traynor also said that if Ansbacher wished, he would take the Hamilton Ross accounts off the Ansbacher books by the end of the month. This is what happened. Traynor told IIB to move funds which had been in Ansbacher pooled accounts to accounts in the name of Hamilton Ross. Clients who up to then had been clients of Ansbacher, now became clients of Hamilton Ross. Most of them knew nothing of this and had never heard of Hamilton Ross. By 30 September 1992, the memorandum accounts being kept in Dublin by Collery were being reconciled with accounts kept in the name of Hamilton Ross in the Cayman Islands. The non-Hamilton Ross accounts remained with Ansbacher.

The movement of the Hamilton Ross accounts out of Ansbacher would, in time, prove to be significant for the clients, because their money, which up to then had been held in the name of a major international banking group, was now in the control of a Cayman Islands company which no-one had ever heard of, and which had no reserves at all. Their money had gone from an international banking group to a firm run by one or two men in a hired office.

Other Irish Ansbacher business remained on the IIB books. Much of this was trust business, and it included the huge John Byrne account. However, the Ansbacher group was generally unhappy with the Traynor operation and was winding down its involvement in Dublin. Some of Traynor's former clients had closed down their accounts to avail of the 1993 tax amnesty. O'Reilly-Hyland, as we have seen, closed his because of difficulties with Lloyds. Others were to close their accounts after Traynor's death, as their involvement had, from their point of view, been with Traynor rather than any particular bank.

There was another reason why the business was being wound down. In January 1993, the Ansbacher group was bought by First National Bank of South Africa (FNBSA). FNBSA had no interest in being involved in the type of business Traynor had developed in Dublin. Traynor and Furze were allowed to stay on the board of the Cayman bank (in Furze's case until 1995) only because it was thought that the resignation or dismissal of a chairman and an executive director would be damaging to the bank's reputation.

In May 1993, a Cayman trust called the Poinciana Trust was established by Traynor, with Furze acting as trustee. Traynor already had a Cayman trust and it seems that the assets of this earlier trust may have been placed with Poinciana. Among the assets assigned to Poinciana were the Cayman companies, Hamilton Ross Co Ltd and Poinciana Fund Ltd. The beneficiaries were to be Traynor, his wife and his family. Because of these facts, the inspectors concluded that Hamilton Ross was owned by Traynor, even before the establishment of the trust when the shares were held in the name of John Furze.

In the last years of Des Traynor's life, therefore, the people who were now in charge of the Cayman bank he had founded and grown, were unhappy with what he had developed and had moved him out of the business because he was considered untrustworthy. This had been done in a confidential way so as not to raise any suspicions. Very few people knew that the high regard with which Traynor was held in business circles generally, was not shared by his colleagues in Ansbacher Cayman. Traynor was still considered by many to be a force in a Cayman Islands bank, and some of his closest acquaintances who were also clients were entirely unaware that the money they had been giving him over the years was now being managed by John Furze in an independent capacity, and not as an employee of a Cayman bank.

It seems that many clients were never told what would happen in the event of Traynor's sudden death. Collery has said that the matter was never raised with him by Traynor. Like his good friend Haughey, Traynor liked to keep his business to himself, telling various people what they needed to know but compartmentalising each person's knowledge so that they could not see the overall picture. Collery knew a lot of what was going on, Williams less. Field-Corbett knew something of what was going on and was about to become more involved. IIB Bank was having ongoing dealings with Traynor, Ansbacher Cayman, Hamilton Ross and Poinciana Fund, but was unaware of what exactly lay behind this.

Traynor's old friend from Haughey Boland, Jack Stakelum, knew quite a bit about what was going on. Stakelum had left Haughey Boland in 1975 and set up a business called Business Enterprises Ltd. Before doing so, he discussed the matter with Traynor. His idea was to provide financial advice to business people and companies, and this is what he did. As a part of this operation he began to place clients' money with Traynor. He told the inspectors that he only did this when asked by clients if he knew somewhere they could place funds. This business started within a year of Stakelum leaving Haughey Boland.

Stakelum said that he knew the money he gave Traynor was held offshore but didn't know exactly where. Interestingly, he set up a structure around this practice which mirrored that which was set up by Traynor when he was in G&M, and later when the deposits were in IIB. Stakelum set up a non-interest earning account with AIB which he used as a kind of float. If someone wanted to put some Irish money in their offshore account he placed it in the float. If someone wanted to take Irish money out he took it from the float. He kept 'memorandum accounts' to monitor who owned what. The float meant that he didn't have to be making a lot of ongoing foreign exchange transactions. The AIB account was non-interest earning so that it would not have to be reported to the Revenue.

The float was used for smaller transactions. For larger ones the withdrawals were made from the Ansbacher accounts in G&M. Stakelum did not open a new account with Traynor for every client, but kept his clients' money in 'hotpotch' or pooled accounts where he knew who owned what, but where Traynor only knew it was money belonging to clients of Stakelum. Once again, this is an example of Ansbacher having clients whose identities were not known. In this case it seems that they were not even known to Traynor.

Stakelum's clients were given the balances on their accounts orally, and not by way of statements. No receipts were ever asked for, or given, by him or his clients. Everything was done on trust. Sometimes loans from G&M were secured for Stakelum's clients, with offshore money being used for cash backing. When, in 1989, Stakelum became unhappy with the kind of service he was receiving from G&M, he moved his clients' offshore accounts to AIB in Jersey. By this time, of course, Traynor had left G&M.

In late 1991, Haughey Boland became part of the much larger Deloitte & Touche group. Traynor was unhappy with the prospect of the bill-paying service operated for Haughey by Haughey Boland continuing within such a large organsation. He and Paul Carty of Haughey Boland met with Stakelum and discussed the matter over lunch. It was agreed that Stakelum would take on the work. Stakelum set up a number of facilities to deal with the service, including getting his bank to supply him with cheques which had a 'microdot' on them to identify the account he was using, instead of Stakelum's name or that of his company. He did this so that people who received cheques in settlement of Haughey's bills would not know where the money was coming from.

When Stakelum needed money in relation to the Haughey bill-paying service, he contacted Traynor. Traynor sent him the money from the Ansbacher Deposits. After Traynor's death, Stakelum continued this service for Haughey, sourcing the money from the Ansbacher Deposits by way of Collery.

The inspectors used their powers to instruct Stakelum to identify clients whose funds he had placed with Ansbacher by way of

Traynor. Those identified included William, Thomas and Margaret Clifford, William and Thomas being the brothers who were in business in Tralee with John Byrne.

Ansbacher Cayman was now under the ownership of the First National Bank of South Africa, and was no longer interested in the Traynor/Irish business. Byrne, however, was different in that he had huge loans out from IIB, backed by hypothecated funds from the Cayman Islands amounting to millions of pounds. Whether he, or the trusts he'd established, had further money on top of this on deposit in the Cayman Islands with Ansbacher is not known. The two trusts he had established were still being managed by Ansbacher, and the companies the trusts owned were still active when Byrne was interviewed by the inspectors in January 2001.

Furze was semi-detached from Ansbacher and running Hamilton Ross himself when Traynor died. He ran the company from small offices he rented on the edge of George Town, along with a friend and new business partner, an American called Barry Benjamin. Furze knew more about Ansbacher's Irish business than anyone else, though of course he did not know the clients nearly as well as Traynor, who knew many of them personally. When Furze suffered what was to be a fatal heart attack in 1997, he was rushed to Miami for medical care. Benjamin told the *Irish Times* that before Furze left for Florida, he told him who to take orders from in relation to Hamilton Ross. Benjamin would not say who this person was. 'That will never come out,' he said.

Traynor had a photographic memory, was discreet, 'honest' and efficient. He was running a secret bank into which he sucked the affairs of people he came into contact with. When he died, many of these people didn't know where to turn. They didn't even know where their money was.

At Traynor's funeral Haughey met with Furze, the only encounter ever between the two men, Haughey later told the Moriarty Tribunal.

Collery may have been introduced to Haughey, who was told that Collery would from now on be looking after his accounts. The truth about this is not clear because Catherine Butler, the secretary who worked for Haughey when he was Taoiseach, had copied out his personal phone book so she could make calls for him, and Collery's number was among those listed. As Haughey had left office before Traynor's death, this would seem to indicate that Haughey had reason to contact Collery before May 1994. Perhaps Traynor had given him the number but it had never been used. Haughey's phone book also included numbers for Williams and for John Guinness, and Catherine Butler told the Moriarty Tribunal that she frequently lined up calls from Haughey to Williams and Traynor when Haughey was Taoiseach.

A few of Traynor's former associates and colleagues attended the funeral wondering what they would do now with the money they'd given to him. One person who didn't know what to do was Tony Barry, the chief executive of CRH. He later asked Sam Field-Corbett if there was any money left in his account, which was much depleted by this time. Barry knew Field-Corbett and Traynor were close, but he is not sure if it was he who approached Field-Corbett after Traynor's death, or the other way around. He told the inspectors he may have said to Field-Corbett: 'By the way Sam, I don't know but I believe I still may have an account and it was opened with Mr Traynor. Do you know how these things worked?' Or he might have been approached by Field-Corbett who said: 'By the way, I think you may still have some money in an account which Mr Collery told me about.' His dealings with the account were after that done by way of Field-Corbett. When he eventually closed the account there was a balance of £4,000 in it. Field-Corbett handed it over to him in cash.

Thomas Killeen, the general practitioner who lived next door to the Traynors, thinks he may have met Furze and Collery in Traynor's home in the days after Traynor's death. Collery, he told the inspectors, called to his home two or three or four days after Traynor's death. He may have met him in Traynor's house at the time of Traynor's death and before the visit by Collery to his home. 'I cannot remember now, but I know that this man introduced himself. I also met another man called John Furze in Traynor's about two or three days after Mr Traynor's death... I have an idea I may have met Collery there, but it was intimated to me that Pádraig Collery was the man who would be dealing with this after that.' As well as dealing with Collery, he also dealt with Sam Field-Corbett. 'If I needed a cheque, I either rang one or the other of them. As far as I remember, it was Mr Field-Corbett that used to [...] I only had communications with him maybe twice, or three times at the very, very most. He would arrange to have a cheque delivered to me or I would pick up a cheque.' He would pick up cheques at Field-Corbett's offices on Winetavern Street.

The Oppermanns had no idea where their money was, and when Traynor died they were at a loss as to how to get it. Eventually they contacted Williams at the CRH offices and told her about their account and how they wanted to close it. She was able to help them. She told them that she would have the account closed and the money could be collected at an address she gave them. They collected the money from Sam Field-Corbett's offices on Winetavern Street.

Arthur Gibney, the architect who had worked with Traynor on the Fitzwilliam Lawn Tennis Club deal, had rarely gone near the account Traynor put £25,000 into in the late 1970s. By the early 1990s it had grown to £100,000 plus, though Gibney had no idea what the balance was. During the late 1980s and early 1990s Gibney did some work on Traynor's house from time to time, every year or two, and he began to make small cash withdrawals. 'He would ask me, "Do you want money?", and I would say, "Yes".' Traynor would then telephone him in a few days and Gibney would drop into Traynor's CRH offices or into Traynor's Howth Road home, and collect a few thousand pounds in cash. After Traynor's death Gibney contacted Williams and asked her what he should do about his account. Gibney was told to contact Collery but had difficulty doing so, so he got in contact with Sam Field-Corbett. A new line of access was opened up and the occasional cash withdrawals continued.

Barbara Breen, the businesswoman who had lived close to the Traynors when she was young, met Collery on the day Traynor died, but it seems that nothing was said about the fund Thomas McLaughlin had created for her at Traynor's urging. Later, Breen approached Stakelum, because Stakelum was a colleague and an advisor to McLoughlin's company, Merops, and because she knew Stakelum and Traynor had been friends. She did not know that Stakelum knew about the money and, in fact, had been told by Traynor never to discuss the matter with Stakelum. 'We would have told him that Mr Traynor had been given money... but we didn't know where the money was so we couldn't tell him where it was.' She thought Stakelum appeared not to know anything about it. However, later withdrawals from the fund were made by way of Stakelum. After the discovery of the deposits in 1997, the money was moved from Ansbacher to an account with Anglo Irish Bank in the Republic, in McLoughlin's name. Breen said she remembered McLoughlin saying at the time that the fund would have grown more substantially if he had put the money into a building society instead of giving it to Traynor. 'That was something he felt very strongly about.' McLoughlin died in 2000. The inspectors decided in their report that McLoughlin's lodgement with Ansbacher had not made Breen a client of Ansbacher.

Gerry Hickey, the solicitor, Fianna Fáil supporter, and CRH and New Ireland Assurance director, who had placed money with Traynor after completing a property deal in Abbey Street, dealt with Collery after Traynor's death. He told the inspectors: 'What happened was, as far as I know, after Des Traynor died in 1994 an awful lot of people withdrew money from the Cayman accounts.' How Hickey could have known this is not clear. He was not questioned about the comment.

16

Discovery

I n early 1997, a group of lawyers gathered in some rooms in Dublin Castle to consider the task they had been assigned by the Oireachtas: Which members of the Oireachtas between 1986 and 1996 had been given money by Ben Dunne and how much had been given? Although it wasn't stated in their terms of reference, the principal job they had was in relation to one politician, Charles Haughey. Had he been given more than £1 million, as reported by the *Irish Times* some months earlier? Haughey was saying nothing. The issue for the lawyers was where to start.

One of their number had pinned a photograph from a newspaper on the office wall. It showed the line-up for St Vincent's GAA club from decades earlier. The club was a famous one, providing many of the players who would form 'Heffo's Army' in the 1970s, the Dublin team which became a powerful force in Gaelic football. In the photograph with the other young players was a young Noel Fox, who had gone on to pursue a successful career in accountancy and business. He had become a financial adviser to Ben Dunne and Dunnes Stores, was a partner in Oliver Freaney & Co, a major accountancy firm, and was an acquaintance of Charles Haughey. The reason the photograph was pinned to the wall was unclear even to the lawyers. Somehow they thought it might be a clue.

The lawyers set about their work unaware that they were being watched, not only by Haughey but also by Traynor's former clients.

Already, highly confidential instructions were being sent by some of these people to their contacts in Dublin, on foot of which millions of pounds was removed from IIB Bank on Merrion Square. Some of the money was being moved to other Dublin banks. More was being sent all the way to the Cayman Islands. Secret meetings were taking place to discuss what the tribunal lawyers knew, what they would do next, and how much they might find out. Haughey was holding secret meetings with Dunne's solicitor, Noel Smyth, seeking insight into what the tribunal lawyers knew and what they might discover. If he had come out with his hands up it might have prevented the tribunal from discovering the Ansbacher Deposits. Associates of his say he was terrified, terrified of being discovered, terrified of being labelled crooked and mendacious, which he was, instead of superior and patriotic, which he also was. He cared hugely about his reputation and what he saw as his place in Irish history. Some people urged him to confess but the habits of a lifetime were too hard to overcome. As always, he played for high stakes. Others could look out for themselves.

Ansbacher bank in the Cayman Islands was watching developments. It appointed a Dublin barrister to discreetly monitor events and report back to it. Furze was monitoring events. He was reading the *Irish Times* every day, pulling it up on the Internet. He was making inquiries of his old pals in Dublin, his co-conspirators. He was shifting money for his old customers, pulling it back to the Caribbean where it might be safer than in a Dublin bank, or at least harder for the Irish authorities to snatch. The conspiracy of a lifetime was in danger of being discovered and he was feeling the strain. In a few months it would kill him.

Since December 1996, the Cayman banker had known that the net was closing on him and his life's work. Furze had been identified in a very simple way. After it was reported that Haughey had received more than £1 million from Ben Dunne, the media kept chipping away at the story. It was learned that money intended for Haughey had been lodged to bank accounts in London in the name of a John Furze. No-one had ever heard of Furze and at first people thought it was a fictitious name. Then, Peter Murtagh, a senior journalist with the *Irish Times* and one of the authors of a book about Haughey, *The Boss*, came up with an idea. In 1997 the data available over the Internet was nothing compared to what it is now. The Haughey story had been broken by Cliff Taylor, then the finance editor with the *Irish Times*, and Murtagh, a former *Guardian* journalist, gave Taylor the name of a man who worked in the *Guardian's* library in London. Taylor contacted this person and, saying he been referred by Murtagh, asked for a favour. The name John Furze was keyed into the newspaper's computerised library filings system. Two entries came up. One was for a Cayman Islands banker who'd received a MBE from the Queen in 1988 for his work for the community on the Cayman Islands.

A finance reporter, Barry O'Keeffe, was dispatched by Taylor to the Caribbean. It was December 1996, a week before Christmas. O'Keeffe surprised Furze by arriving at his doorstep. The banker, a middle-aged man with a gravelly voice and a lined, worn face, explained that the Cayman Islands had strict confidentiality laws and said he could not give O'Keeffe any information. However, given that O'Keeffe had travelled so far, he agreed to meet with him the following day in his office. It was to be the only interview Furze would ever give, to journalists or to lawyers. He said little, and some of what he did say was untrue.

The McCracken Tribunal was established on 7 February 1997. Mr Justice McCracken set up office in Dublin Castle along with registrar Annette O'Connell, and a solicitor from the Chief State Solicitor's office, John Lawless. They were soon joined by barristers Michael Collins SC, Denis McCullough SC, and Anthony Aston, and an assistant solicitor from the Chief State Solicitor's office, Joanne Dwyer.

One of the tribunal's first and more obvious ports of call was Ben Dunne. It sought information from him, and on 24 March 1997 received a lengthy statement and supporting documentation. Dunne had been involved in a bitter legal dispute with his siblings and the Dunnes Trust in 1994, during which he had had cause to draft various legal documents outlining extremely controversial allegations he would make should the dispute ever go forward for hearing. One such document was a reply to a notice for particulars. It gave very precise information concerning payments to Haughey. In relation to a payment of £471,000 sterling, it was stated that the money was sent on 14 July 1988 from Switzerland to Barclays Bank plc, Knightsbridge, London, 'for credit to account number 40384976 in the name of John A Furze'.

Faced with Haughey's lack of co-operation, the tribunal was left with no option but to follow the money trail. Dunne's statement of particulars gave it its first port of call. The cheques which had been written out for Haughey's benefit contained stamps on the front and back showing when and where they had been lodged. The tribunal went to the High Court in London and to the Grand Court of the Cayman Islands with letters of request. These are legal requests under the Evidence (Proceedings in Other Jurisdictions) Act 1975 of the United Kingdom, an act which applies in the Cayman Islands, as well as in the UK.

On 1 May 1997, evidence was taken in private from witnesses on behalf of London-based Guinness Mahon & Co, the Henry Ansbacher group and Barclays Bank plc. Further evidence was taken from witnesses from these banks, and from the Royal Bank of Scotland a week later.

Meanwhile the tribunal had been meeting and interviewing people from G&M bank and IIB Bank in Dublin. The money trail, though it went through some complicated loops in London, seemed to head towards both of these merchant banks, leading the tribunal to conclude that whoever the beneficiary or beneficiaries of the Dunne money were, they had connections with these banks. Furthermore, in both instances the money was lodged to accounts in the Dublin banks which were in the name of Ansbacher (Cayman) Ltd, the Cayman Islands bank. So, as is the way with such matters, they began to pry into Ansbacher Cayman.

IIB Bank knew little about Ansbacher other than that it was a Cayman bank which it did business with. However, the same was not true of G&M. Sandra Kells of G&M explained to the tribunal that Ansbacher (Cayman) was in fact a former subsidiary of G&M which had been founded by Des Traynor in the early 1970s. The tribunal had been told that it was Traynor who had, by way of Noel Fox, sought money from Dunne for Haughey. The tribunal issued orders of discovery – orders which have the power and authority of the High Court – against the two banks. It got heaps of material in response. The IIB material was not of much interest. The material received from G&M, however, was different.

The tribunal learned that Ansbacher business with G&M during much of the period being examined had formed a significant proportion of the Dublin bank's overall business. On the face of it it was not clear why this should be so. However, the material discovered from G&M included one key document, the internal audit report of G&M conducted for its London parent in 1989, and this document shed some light on what was going on. The situation was not particularly easy to understand, but had obviously been the cause of some concern to those who had carried out the 1989 audit. Furthermore, the deposits placed by Ansbacher with G&M at the time of the audit amounted to nearly £38 million, or 35 per cent of all deposits held by the bank.

Two key points outlined in the audit report were: that coded accounts held in an inaccessible part of the G&M computer were related to money for Irish clients which was nominally 'offshore'; and that someone identified as DPC had sole charge of Ansbacher's deposits with G&M, and was the only person with access to the associated coded accounts maintained on the inaccessible part of the G&M computer.

The tribunal asked G&M who DPC was, and was told that it was Pádraig Collery, who no longer worked with the bank. He was soon tracked down and invited to Dublin Castle. The tribunal lawyers were trying to match the evidence coming from the banks in London with the evidence coming from the banks in Dublin. At times there were conflicts and the matter was not at all easy. The lawyers thought that Collery was the administrative expert in relation to the bank's operations and would be able to explain what was going on. Collery, of course, was much more than a computer expert or a senior administrator. Since the death of Traynor in 1994 he was the key Irish figure involved in operating the Ansbacher Deposits, and had been Traynor's key Dublin deputy since at least the late 1980s. The lawyers did not know this and Collery, a lifelong banker whom people trusted to deal with their affairs in confidence, was not going to go out of his way to assist a public tribunal. The lawyers found him to be of little use.

The witnesses in London had provided further insight into G&M's relationship with Ansbacher. A witness from Ansbacher's parent in London, Henry Ansbacher & Co, Peter Greenhalgh, said that when it bought Guinness Mahon Cayman Trust it felt that it was basically buying 'an Irish operation'. He also said that 'memorandum accounts' were kept to record who owned what within the general or pooled Ansbacher accounts in Dublin. Collins, who was taking evidence from Greenhalgh, said that he didn't understand the term, 'memorandum accounts'. Greenhalgh explained that memorandum accounts were ones which were not kept on the books of the bank. They were 'shadow' accounts held elsewhere. Memorandum accounts, held in Dublin outside the bank, held the key to who owned what in the pooled Ansbacher accounts.

As well as this background evidence concerning the Cayman bank and its relationship with its former parent in Dublin, the tribunal lawyers asked specific questions about the amounts they were trying to trace to see if they went to Haughey.

It was not the tribunal's job to investigate the relationship between Ansbacher and G&M, or whether a raft of Irish customers were using G&M to nominally lodge money with an offshore bank. The lawyers were trying to establish whether Haughey got Dunne's money, but they were finding this to be difficult because of how the Ansbacher Deposits worked.

It was hard to show what happened to money which went into the pooled Ansbacher accounts if you didn't have access to the Cayman bank's records or the records kept by Collery. The tribunal lawyers went through a laborious process of looking at a huge number of bank statements to see if they could spot particular amounts of money going into the pooled account and coming out again. On occasion they struck it lucky.

For instance, the first payment looked at, £182,603 sterling, was lodged to an account called the 'sundry sub-account of Guinness Mahon Cayman Trust', on 17 December 1987. The money had been sent to Guinness Mahon & Co, London, on 8 December. On 15 December, £204,055.87 was withdrawn from the GMCT sundry sub-account in G&M, and lodged to an account in the same bank in the name of Amiens Investments Ltd. The Irish pound amount was the then exact equivalent of £182,630 sterling. The sundry sub-account was the pooled account already referred to.

By catching this correlation between a lodgement to, and a withdrawal from, the pooled account, the lawyers were led to the Amiens account. Examination of this account found that £105,000 had gone from it to ACC Bank on 2 December 1987. When the tribunal followed this amount to ACC Bank, they found that it had been lodged to an account in the name of Charles Haughey. (Someone had earlier ribbed the lawyers that they would never discover money being lodged to an account in Haughey's name.)

Further examination of the Amiens account by the tribunal lawyers showed that on 18 December 1987, £30,000 was debited from the account. Four days later, £10,000 was debited. On that same date, 22 December 1987, £59,000 was withdrawn from the account in cash. No receipts existed for the withdrawal, meaning that the money was withdrawn by someone very well known to the bank.

The ACC money, the two debits and the cash withdrawal totalled exactly the amount credited to the Amiens account from the GMCT pooled account and, therefore, the amount from Dunne which had been lodged to the pooled account.

G&M was not a retail bank, meaning it didn't normally have customers calling in and making cash withdrawals. It did have an across-the-counter cash service if required. Customers wanting large amounts of cash would have to order them in advance, and the bank would in turn order up the money so it would have it ready for collection. The lawyers noticed that there were lots of cash withdrawals being made from the Ansbacher accounts they were examining. G&M staff told them that this money was generally collected from the lobby of the bank. It was a strange thing to be happening to money which was ostensibly owned by a bank located half-way around the globe. The lawyers were becoming more and more convinced that transactions involving the Ansbacher accounts in fact reflected the transactions of Irish individuals. This view was reinforced by the fact that a lot of the payments across the accounts were to pay credit card bills.

The orders of discovery issued by the tribunal had produced originals and copies of notes sent to IIB Bank and G&M concerning money held in the Ansbacher accounts. Mostly these notes were sent by Joan Williams. The notes showed money being lodged and withdrawn but gave no clue as to whose money exactly was involved. Williams was interviewed but proved to be of as little value to the tribunal's inquiries as Collery had been.

Nevertheless, as their inquiries progressed, the tribunal lawyers became more and more confident that the picture they were forming of the Ansbacher operation was correct. At first they felt they would never be able to work out where the Dunne money went unless they could get access to the records held by Ansbacher on the Cayman Islands. The money disappeared into the thick undergrowth of the pooled Ansbacher accounts and the only way to trace what happened to particular amounts, they felt, would be to get access to the records which traced those particular amounts. But their efforts to get the Cayman bank to co-operate in this regard, led them in time to re-assess that view.

In its request to the Grand Court of the Cayman Islands the tribunal asked that it be allowed to take evidence from officers of Ansbacher Cayman, including John Furze and John Collins. Furze vigorously opposed the application. The other parties told the court that they would consider themselves bound by any orders made in response to the objection by Furze. The Cayman courts administer the strict confidentiality laws introduced in the 1970s which led to the islands becoming one of the most successful financial centres in the world. In essence, permission must be had from the courts before confidential business information can be disclosed to a third party, and infringement of the law is a criminal offence. The tribunal, in seeking to gather evidence in the Cayman Islands, was always fighting an uphill battle.

Mr Justice McCracken, Collins, McCullough and Lawless travelled to the Cayman Islands for their hearing in the Grand Court. They had engaged an Irish lawyer with a practice on the Cayman Islands, Charlie Quin of Quin & Hampson, who had in turn engaged a London QC, Anthony Bueno. They set themselves up in a large office in the Quin & Hampson premises, poring over the large amount of documentation they had brought with them. A large window on one side of the room looked out on the George Town harbour and the blue Caribbean. At one stage they thought they might just call on Furze in his home in an exclusive development called Governor's Harbour. The lawyers went as far as the gates which led into the development and then, deciding against going any further, took a photograph of themselves instead. They never got to meet, or even see, the Cayman banker.

The application was not successful, failing on the grounds that, while the Cayman confidentiality law provided for co-operation with cases being taken by higher courts abroad, the court did not consider the tribunal to be a higher court. The decision was not given immediately. The court heard the case, in camera, over three days in a small air-conditioned room. On 27 May the judge, Mr Justice Patterson, said that he was reserving the application.

In the course of the action, however, it seems that the tribunal team did manage to glean some information from their opposing numbers or, rather, managed to form the impression that they were on the right track. At this stage the lawyers had a very incomplete view of something which was complex in its details, clandestine, and hitherto unknown to them as a phenomenon. The Ansbacher arrangement was an offshore bank which was not offshore, it was a massive, secret financial service run, not only for Charles Haughey, but also for many of the most senior business figures of Haughey's generation. No one person had sat down with them and explained what was going on, nor had anyone confirmed to them that their suspicions were correct.

The lawyers, as is their wont, tried to cut a deal with the opposition. They sought information or guidance from the bank or from Furze, in return for absolute confidentiality in regard to the fact of this co-operation, plus the withdrawal of their application to the Cayman courts. This was a very delicate manoeuvre because if the bank or Furze went too far, they would be committing a criminal offence under Cayman law. A fine line would have to be drawn.

The lawyers were unsuccessful, but the exercise proved rewarding. The opposing side, perhaps inadvertently, confirmed to the McCracken team that they were forming a correct picture of what they were discovering. They did this, not by offering information or viewpoints, but simply by not expressing astonishment or bafflement or simply by not disagreeing with statements made by the tribunal team when they, the tribunal lawyers, were seeking co-operation. A key issue, it seems, in all of this, was the extent to which records of what had been happening existed back in Ireland. While the delicate negotiations were continuing in the Cayman Islands, considerably less delicate inquiries, and demands, were being made in Dublin. Pádraig Collery was the focus.

Collery met in private with the tribunal team following the discovery of the audit report which mentioned his name. The meeting led to very little information being disclosed. However, from then on a clearer picture began to emerge of how important a role Collery played in the operation of the Ansbacher Deposits. On 16 May Collery was interviewed again. This was just before the trip to the Cayman Islands. Already, the tribunal suspected that Collery had key documentation concerning the deposits. An order of discovery was made. The bulk of the tribunal team then headed off for the Caribbean, but kept in contact with developments back in Dublin.

Collery was fighting hard to keep secret the memorandum accounts, what they contained and, most importantly, the identities of the people who were the owners of the money in the coded accounts. He sought legal advice as to what documents he had to discover and what notice he had to give the Cayman companies which were the owners of the originals of the documents he had. He questioned how he might balance banker/client confidentiality and the tribunal's order. The order was challenged in terms of its breadth, and clarification was sought in regard to the tribunal's terms of reference. But Collery was fighting a losing battle. His choice was stark: comply with the order or risk going to jail.

On 25 June, Collery supplied the tribunal with hundreds of documents including bank statements, memos, and notes and letters which had been written to him by Traynor. There were letters or notes telling Collery to debit or credit particular coded accounts in the memorandum accounts. These were the key instructions needed to enable Collery to track the changing ownership of the monies pooled in the key Ansbacher accounts. The instructions never referred to names. They said: Debit AA/1 £10,000 sterling; Credit S3 £50,000 sterling, and so on. There were also short notes written on the copy instructions, including many references to JJS, who was to be given money debited from particular debited accounts. No one knew who, or what, JJS was. There was no obvious mention of the tribunal's target, Haughey. Williams was asked to shed light on what was going on but was of little assistance.

A week before the tribunal was due to reconvene in public session, there came the big breakthrough. As they leafed through the hundreds and hundreds of useless documents they'd gathered, the lawyers came across one with a scribbled note on it, written by Williams: 'By hand to CJH, 30th of November 1993.' The note was written on the bottom of a letter concerning the withdrawal of £25,000 sterling from one of the coded accounts, a deutschmark account with the code S9. In all the documentation they had been given, it was the only reference to CJH. It had to be Haughey.

The tribunal followed the draft. It was lodged to an ACC Bank account in Haughey's name, a farm management account to do with his Kinsealy estate. It seemed Haughey must have needed the money in a hurry and had got on to Traynor. Traynor had given the task to Williams, who had secured the draft from IIB bank and had it couriered to Haughey. Whatever the facts behind it, the note was strong evidence that the S9 account was Haughey's.

There were other S-coded accounts detailed in the documentation the tribunal had gathered. A list of the accounts had the letters HC opposite the one coded S9. Could HC be Charles Haughey? It had to be. Furthermore, the same letters, HC, appeared opposite the S8 account on the same list. Collery was called in for another interview. Confronted with the evidence as to who owned the S8 and S9 accounts, he admitted that he knew that the accounts held money for Haughey. The JJS who usually received the money drawn from the accounts, he revealed, was the accountant, Jack Stakelum. Stakelum was contacted.

The day after they met with Collery in Dublin Castle, the tribunal met with Stakelum in the Four Courts. Stakelum quickly filled in the tribunal as to his involvement. In January 1992 he had started operating a bill-paying service for Haughey, settling his bills and receiving the money needed to do so from Traynor. After Traynor's death in 1994, Stakelum said, Collery had taken over the role. Stakelum had taken on the job from Haughey Boland at the time Haughey Boland was joining with Deloitte & Touche. An order of discovery was issued for the documentation held by Stakelum. Deloitte & Touche were contacted and a senior partner there, Paul Carty, began to assist the tribunal in its inquiries.

The picture was being filled in. The money from Dunne had gone into general Ansbacher accounts. The S8 and S9 accounts held money owned by Haughey. The two accounts were used by Haughey to defray the cost of his extraordinarily lavish lifestyle, and the tribunal was able to document amounts being debited from the accounts to be credited to Haughey Boland or Stakelum. From records held by Haughey Boland the tribunal established the level of expenditure by Haughey during the period from 1 August 1988 to 31 January 1991. It totalled £708,850. After Stakelum took over, a similar level of expenditure continued. It was more than enough to cover the Dunne donations.

The tribunal's function was to trace payments from Dunne to politicians, not to investigate the Ansbacher Deposits, so its inquiries into Traynor's secret bank now came to an end. Furthermore, with the evidence mounting against Haughey, the former Taoiseach admitted that he'd received the Dunne money, and that he'd been lying all along.

This admission by Haughey (of what had already been established) came too late to prevent the whole Ansbacher scenario being disclosed to the public. On 30 June, Denis McCullough SC stood up in George's Hall, in Dublin Castle, at the re-opening of public sessions of the tribunal. Judge McCracken asked him to 'bring people up-to-date on what has been happening since we last sat'. McCullough gave a very broad outline of what had been discovered, during the course of which he dubbed the secret accounts run by Traynor as 'the Ansbacher Deposits'.

The tribunal soon completed its work, finishing on a dramatic note with the examination of Haughey, and his being booed by the crowd in Castle Yard as he emerged afterwards. Haughey had accepted that he had been given in excess of £1 million by Dunne. The process of proving this had led to the discovery of the Ansbacher Deposits. Because the tribunal had been unable to show the money going directly into a Haughey account or accounts, the tribunal had had to explain in public its reasoning for concluding that Haughey had received the money. Hence the need to go into some detail about Traynor, Collery, Furze, the Cayman Islands, G&M and IIB Bank. None of this had anything to do with the tribunal's terms of reference, and if Haughey had simply admitted receiving the money, and using it to feed his bill-paying service, then perhaps the tribunal would not have had reason to examine the matter at all.

With the cat finally out of the bag, the clamour began for a full-blown inquiry into the Ansbacher Deposits and the naming of all the depositors. The Fianna Fáil/PD government, led by Bertie Ahern, was loathe to have any such inquiry and the main opposition party, Fine Gael, was equally cool on the issue. The Ansbacher controversy became separated from the issue of payments to Haughey, in part, no doubt, because Ben Dunne was not an Ansbacher depositor. When the new tribunal, the Moriarty (Payments to Politicians) Tribunal was put in place, it was charged with investigating payments to Haughey (and Michael Lowry), and with inquiring into whether any more politicians had money in the Ansbacher Deposits. Two more were to be found, Denis Foley, from Fianna Fáil, and Hugh Coveney, from Fine Gael.

17

What We'll Never Know

In the history of post-independence Ireland, Mary Harney has wielded more political power than any other woman. She was born in Co. Galway in 1953, but grew up in south Dublin. She attended Trinity College and while there came to the attention of the then Taoiseach, Jack Lynch. In August 1977, when she was appointed by Lynch to the Senate, she was the youngest-ever member of the upper house. She has been in politics all her life.

Harney left Fianna Fáil and joined the Progressive Democrats in 1985 when that party was set up by the long-time Haughey opponent within Fianna Fáil, Des O'Malley. When O'Malley retired as leader of the party Harney replaced him. She formed a government with Bertie Ahern in early 1997 and took on the roles of Tánaiste and Minister for Enterprise, Trade and Employment. The linked issues of enterprise, low taxes and reduced public expenditure have been her main political projects. The government she and Ahern ran slashed a range of taxes, not only income tax but also Corporation Tax and Capital Gains Tax. A programme to reduce Corporation Tax to 12.5 per cent, close to, if not the lowest in the European Union, was put in progress, while Capital Gains Tax was reduced from 40 per cent to 20 per cent.

The attraction of foreign multinationals to Ireland by way of low taxes has angered many of Ireland's European partners, who see it as a case of the country they gave so much assistance to using tax competition in a way that threatens the European social model. Harney sees low taxes as being a spur to enterprise which, in turn, she believes to be the greatest way of addressing the issue of poverty. The best security against poverty, she says, is a job. It is an interesting debate, and while the lowering of taxes during an unprecedented boom in Ireland created no revenue difficulties for the exchequer, post-boom the question arose as to how the exchequer would cope in less buoyant periods. At the heart of the matter is the kind of society which will be built in the Republic.

This sort of serious politics, addressing structural issues which, in turn, shape the kind of society people live in, was what she had in mind when she took on her new role in the Fianna Fáil/PD government in 1997. Investigations into suspected breaches of company law were not high on her list of priorities, but ultimately became a huge issue during the period of that government. Her department oversaw the Companies Acts, which allows for the appointment of authorised officers and inspectors. The former are allowed to inspect the books of a company and to file reports to the Minister, which have to be kept confidential. The latter are more powerful figures who have the right to inspect books and to compel a range of people to give evidence on oath. They report to the High Court and their reports may be published. In the case of both authorised officers and inspectors, the suspected defrauding by a company of its creditors or the collusion by a company in the defrauding of other's creditors, are among the scenarios where a minister could initiate an inquiry. By the end of the 1997/2002 government, Harney had initiated an unprecedented number of inquiries, including those into National Irish Bank, Dunnes Stores, and Garuda Ltd, a company run by the former Fine Gael minister, Michael Lowry.

Harney was in the US on departmental business when the McCracken Report was published in August 1997. It was a groundbreaking moment because the small, clearly written, concise report was in stark contrast to the large Beef Tribunal report written by Mr Justice Hamilton a few years earlier. McCracken reported, simply, that Haughey was given money by Dunne, that this was wrong, and that Haughey had lied to and misled the tribunal and could therefore be guilty of a criminal offence. He sent the tribunal's papers to the DPP and Haughey was later brought before the courts and charged. News of the report was conveyed to Harney in the US. The matters covered in the report included the making of off-the-books payments to Garuda, and the secret backing of loans to Celtic Helicopters. The backing was with money from the Ansbacher Deposits, and in one instance a Celtic Helicopters loan was even paid off with money from the deposits. Harney said to her department's secretary that it should look into these two matters. Authorised officers were appointed to both companies. Gerry Ryan, a civil servant and accountant, was appointed to Celtic Helicopters.

The main reaction to the McCracken Report was centred else-where. The McCracken Tribunal had been an inquiry into payments to politicians by Dunnes Stores/Ben Dunne. Now the demand was for a new tribunal which would investigate Haughey's finances and all payments to him which could be discovered. The government acceded to this but charged that the tribunal should also inquire into the finances of the former Fine Gael minister, Michael Lowry. There were also demands for a full inquiry into the Ansbacher Deposits, but this demand was resisted.

The McCracken Tribunal had revealed that Dunne had given more than £1 million to Haughey; that Des Traynor had been contacting rich people and asking them for money; that Traynor had been looking after Haughey's finances since the 1960s; that Traynor ran a secret onshore/offshore banking system that was used by the 'cream' of the Irish business world; and that Haughey had an Ansbacher account. It was an explosive mix and naturally led to speculation that the Ansbacher Deposits structure lay at the heart of a political/commercial conspiracy which had operated at the heart of Irish society during the Haughey years. There was a feeling that revealing the truth about the Ansbacher Deposits would cast a whole new light on an era. Exposure of the Ansbacher customers would be some type of lifting of the veil, exposing reality in all its shocking detail. The emphasis put on Traynor's secretive tax avoidance/evasion operation went into overdrive and became the focus for many people's sense of grievance arising from the unemployment, emigration and frustration which had been such a feature of the 1970s and 1980s. Posters appeared on walls and lamp posts, 'Jail the Ansbacher Rich'. It was an uncomfortable time for a lot of people.

The Government, however, resisted calls for a full inquiry by the new tribunal into the Ansbacher operation, and the public naming of those who had had deposits with Traynor. They were supported in their resistance by Fine Gael, creating further suspicion and loss of confidence in the political process. There was talk of a flight of capital from the country if any such name and shame process was initiated. Instead, the tribunal was asked to report on any payments from the deposits to politicians, and a number of related policy matters to do with offshore accounts and taxation. By September, the Moriarty Tribunal was established and set about its work. It seemed that the Ansbacher clients were off the hook.

Meanwhile, Gerry Ryan was beavering away looking into the books of Celtic Helicopters. Within months it became clear to him that a full report to Harney would not be possible without getting access to other books which were not the property of Celtic Helicopters and, therefore, to which he had no right of access under law. He held a meeting with Harney in her Kildare Street offices and explained to her how matters were developing. In order to complete his work on Celtic Helicopters, he needed to get at the books of Guinness & Mahon and Irish Intercontinental Bank. Lawyers were called in and the matter was discussed in detail. In essence, the point was this: Ryan's work on Celtic Helicopters indicated that breaches of company law by the two Dublin banks had taken place. Harney decided to appoint Ryan to the two banks, not just to inquire into Celtic Helicopters' dealings with them, but also in relation to the overall operation of their affairs. Soon afterwards, again because of Ryan's work, she appointed him to Ansbacher Cayman and Hamilton Ross. While the Moriarty Tribunal trundled along up in Dublin Castle, at huge expense to the taxpayer, a civil servant in

Harney's department began to dig deep into the Ansbacher Deposits.

The outing of Ansbacher names became a media bloodsport and as the Celtic Tiger boom advanced, so too did the unending speculation about who was on the Ansbacher list. Rumours came and went. Harney spoke publicly of people seeking to put pressure on her to back off. This was a reference to comments made to her in social contexts, sometimes echoing the comments made in the Dáil at the time of the debate on the McCracken Tribunal report, that there would be a flight of capital from the country. Legal representations and protests on behalf of people and companies poured into her office. Politically, she was left alone by her coalition partners, with no-one asking her to back off, no-one trying to get in her way, and no one coming out with enthusiastic support.

During 1988, Pádraig Collery lost his nerve. The Ansbacher controversy was in full swing and he was in the eye of the storm. He was dealing with inquiries from former clients of Traynor's. He was himself the subject of Revenue inquiries and was looking at a huge tax bill which would wipe out all of the money he had earned from his years of secret work on the Ansbacher system. He had been at the centre of the McCracken Tribunal and was now in the sights of the Moriarty Tribunal. He was also about to face the attentions of the High Court inspectors, whom many people were presuming would one day be appointed.

He felt that his home was being watched and that his phone was being bugged. He feared someone would break into or raid his house and steal or take documentation he had stashed there. He'd done something a bit wild in July. At the invitation of Barry Benjamin, the man who'd taken over from Furze, Collery had travelled to the Cayman Islands for a week. He hadn't told the tribunal, even though he was reassuring the tribunal, in private, that he was co-operating fully with it.

Collery was concerned about how matters were unfolding with Hamilton Ross. People were phoning him and saying they couldn't get information about their accounts from Benjamin. He was worried that people would never see their money again, and would hold him responsible, even though he'd had nothing to do with the accounts since around the time of Furze's death in 1997.

When he went to the Cayman Islands in July 1998, Collery went through the books with Benjamin, applying interest to the accounts and bringing the balances up to date as of July 1998. There were 19 Irish accounts still on the Hamilton Ross books. The two men went through the accounts and deducted money from most of them to pay for legal fees totalling £57,000, which had been incurred by Furze a year earlier when he'd resisted the McCracken Tribunal in the Cayman courts. The account holders were not informed or consulted before their money was taken in this way. No money was deducted from the accounts belonging to Collery, Williams or Field-Corbett.

When Collery was leaving the islands at the end of his visit, he brought with him written copies of the various balances on the accounts. This, he thought, would serve as protection if a disgruntled Irish account holder ever sought to sue him. He would use the documents to support his case that nothing had happened to the money up to the time he relinquished responsibility for it around the time of the McCracken Tribunal.

An odd thing about the documents and the whole scenario at this stage was that the accounts he brought home with him contained a name which had not yet been revealed to the Moriarty Tribunal by Collery. Denis Foley was, at this time, still a Fianna Fáil TD and a member of the Dáil Public Accounts committee. He was even, amazingly, a member of a sub-committee of that committee which was holding a high-profile inquiry into bogus non-resident accounts in Irish banks. At the same time he was fearful that he would be caught out as an Ansbacher depositor. Why, of all the people who had been caught up in the Ansbacher scandal, Collery was protecting Foley has never been adequately explained.

One possible explanation is that at the time of Collery's trip to the Cayman Islands the Ansbacher inspectors had still not been appointed. Therefore, at that time there was no inquiry under way which would necessarily lead to an Ansbacher client being publicly identified – unless the client was a politician. The terms of reference for the Moriarty Tribunal included the naming of politicians who were found to have had dealings with the Ansbacher Deposits, but otherwise it had no role in naming Ansbacher customers. Coveney was already known to the tribunal but not Foley. Was this the reason for concealing Foley? We don't know. What can be said, however, was that even at that late stage there was an attempt to conceal the name of a client.

Collery was afraid that his house would be raided and the documents he was hiding would be discovered by the tribunal, and his secret trip to the Cayman Islands would be thereby revealed. He decided to take the documents down to a house he owned in his native Sligo. While waiting to go on the trip he thought he would leave the documents for a few days with a woman he'd worked with when he was at G&M. He called around to her home and gave her a sealed envelope which he asked her to mind for him for a few days. The woman agreed but then became worried, sought legal advice and, acting on that advice, handed the package over to the tribunal. It contained the statements Collery had brought back to Ireland with him, including one referring to Foley. It was a disastrous development for the TD, whose career ended in disgrace and who, perhaps equally hurtful for him, now found himself being investigated by the Revenue.

This latter aspect of the affair was all the more painful for Foley, in that he was going to have to settle with the Revenue in relation to his offshore money, while not being sure whether he would ever be able to get his money back from the Cayman Islands. So far, this issue has not been resolved. Benjamin will not discuss individuals' affairs, but says that he must have legal proof that money he holds belongs to a particular person before he will deal with any correspondence or contact received. It seems that a number of people are facing the possibility of substantial tax bills, while, at the same time, being unsure as to when, if ever, they will be able to repatriate the money they have on deposit in the Cayman Islands. Benjamin says he is tempted at this stage to give it all away to a charity of his choice.

In time, Ryan reported back to Harney and again there were high-level discussions and the seeking of legal advice. In September 1999 the High Court was asked, on foot of what had been discovered by Ryan, to appoint inspectors to Ansbacher Cayman. The court acceded to the request. It appointed Mr Justice Declan Costello, Noreen Mackey and Paul Rowan. Mackey was a barrister. Rowan was an accountant who had investigated part of the Gallagher group in Northern Ireland following that group's collapse in the 1980s, an investigation which had led to Gallagher being jailed for fraud. Costello was a retired judge and author of the 'Just Society' document produced for Fine Gael in the 1950s. He was to later withdraw from the inquiry for health reasons and was replaced by Judge Sean O'Leary and Michael Cush SC.

The appointment of the inspectors was the move the people who'd been doing business with Traynor had been dreading. The inspectors were appointed under Section 8 of the Companies Act 1990, a section which gave them the power to compel witnesses to attend and give evidence before them and which allowed, subject to the decision of the court, for their report to be published. The terms of reference given to the inspectors were controversial as they were asked to not only inquire into what the company, Ansbacher, had been up to in Ireland, but also to identify who its Irish-resident clients were, and any other clients of its Irish operation. Many of the clients felt that this was unfair, as the inspectors were, they believed, being appointed under the Companies Acts to inquire not into a company, but into the affairs of particular individuals. One of the problems these people faced, however, was that to take an action against the inspectors, in order to preserve their good name, they would have to openly state in court that they were likely to be named as clients of Ansbacher. Otherwise they would not be able to make the case as they would not be an interested party. This was a key issue.

In fact, later, as the inspectors' work neared completion, two clients tried to take a case against the inspectors' report without revealing their names. Their counsel, Michael Collins SC, the barrister who'd formed part of the McCracken Tribunal's legal team, argued before Mr Justice McCracken in the High Court that if the applicants had to reveal their names, it would defeat the purpose of the application. However, Mr Justice McCracken said justice had to be administered in public and that that included the applicants being named. He pointed out that people accused of criminal offences are named, even though they are at the time presumed innocent. Faced with this decision, the applicants withdrew.

There were in-camera hearings during the course of the inspectors' work, and one in particular where the inspectors sought clarification as to the extent to which they should pry or inquire into the tax affairs of Ansbacher clients. The court told them to limit their inquiries in this regard to identifying the clients, and investigating their affairs to the extent to which it was necessary in order to define the service provided by Ansbacher. In their report, the inspectors said that in the more than 100 cases where they addressed Revenue issues, they did not find one case where a client who had access to his or her Cayman trust by way of deposits made by the trust in a Dublin bank, had made contemporaneous tax returns in relation to the transactions. They cautioned against concluding that everyone named in the report had been guilty of tax evasion, but added; 'There is evidence tending to show that the scheme as operated by Guinness & Mahon and GMCT facilitated the widespread evasion of tax.'

Transcripts of interviews with Ansbacher clients were published in the report. The impression given was that the interviewees believed that the content of the interviews would remain confidential. In some instances assurances were sought in this regard. Usually this was when the interviewee was giving some background detail to his or her dealings with Traynor. In one instance there was a mention of some difficulty among siblings, while another seemed to concern the upkeep of an apartment using Ansbacher money. In general, the feel from the interviews was that the interviewees were speaking with a candidness indicating they did not believe or understand that the transcripts would form part of the final report. How the decision to publish the transcripts was taken is not known.

In fact, the transcripts formed the most interesting part of the report. The Ansbacher inspectors' inquiry was, in many ways, the wrong sort of inquiry to have into the Ansbacher Deposits. It happened by accident and involved the use of a law which was designed to allow for the investigation of suspected breaches of company law by a company. And so the inspectors' inquiry was into whether the company operated here as a bank without a licence to do so from the Central Bank, which it did; whether it evaded tax, which it did; and whether it facilitated the evasion of tax by others, which it did. It was an investigation into an elaborate, though in truth not particularly sophisticated, tax scam. As both Mary Harney and her colleague in the PDs, the Minister for Justice, Michael McDowell, said in the wake of the publication of the inspectors' report, it is inevitable that there were other shows in town during the period concerned. The reason so many people became so interested and concerned about the Ansbacher Deposits was because of the nature of Traynor's relationship with Haughey, yet that was not a concern of the inspectors at all. In fact, Haughey, because of his medical condition, was one of the few clients who was not interviewed and the report, in so far as it dealt with him, was not particularly interesting. The only matter of note was that in his response to the inspectors' preliminary findings, Haughey, through his solicitors, rejected the finding that he was a client of Ansbacher.

The Ansbacher scam was undoubtedly one which was used by people of note in the period during which it was in operation. However, the fact that the inspectors did not, and were not required to, inquire into the political aspects of the overall affair, meant that the report's eventual publication in July 2002 was something of an anti-climax. The public had been expecting the outing of people of note who had not already been identified in the newspapers, but this did not occur. There was talk of judges and hospital consultants and barristers, but that didn't happen and, anyway, if it had it is not clear that it would have made much of a difference. There were already lots of wealthy and privileged people linked to the deposits. Another politician was never going to be named, as the Moriarty Tribunal had already conducted a public investigation into the affairs of politicians linked to Ansbacher. The involvement of Haughey, Coveney and Foley with the accounts was already known.

The closest the report came to dealing with the politics of the time was in the accumulation of detail. The economy awoke from its slumber in the 1960s. Capital taxes were introduced in the 1970s and the big accountancy firms looked for new ways to manage their clients' money. The businessmen and companies who did business with Traynor, Haughey Boland, and the State, while at the same time supporting Fianna Fáil and, in some instances, Haughey personally, were without a doubt 'inside the loop' in a way which was very unhealthy. It was this aspect of the Ansbacher affair which people wanted investigated, but the connection between politics and money was something which only occasionally cast its shadow on the contents of the report. Mostly this occured as a result of brief illuminating comments in the course of the interviews with the clients. What we have now is likely to be as much as we will ever have.

Epilogue

T he Revenue Commissioners are conducting an enormous inquiry into the Ansbacher conspiracy, an inquiry which is leading it to examine the general affairs of those named as Ansbacher clients. For many of these clients the years since 1997 have been difficult ones. Some people, clients and beneficiaries of trusts, have died. It is possible that the strain and ignominy caused by their association with Traynor and Ansbacher may have been a contributory factor in at least some of these deaths. The substantial homes of a number of the bigger names in the Ansbacher list have featured in recent years in the property supplement of the *Irish Times*.

Traynor's wife sold the family home on Howth Road in early 2002 for approximately €2.5 million. The family has stayed silent in relation to all that has befallen them in the years since 1997, although some of the details of Traynor's personal financial affairs are on public record. The documents on file in the Probate Office show that the executors of the estate were Sam Field-Corbett and a relative. The gross size of Traynor's estate was given as £1,739,888, and the net estate as £1,307,664, the difference being accounted for by Capital Gains Tax paid on the disposal of shares. The estate was said to be 'exclusive of what the deceased may have been possessed of, or entitled to, as a trustee and not beneficially'. Stocks and shares were given a value of £889,318, and cash in the bank a value of £689,588. Most of the money in the bank was in the ICS building society and G&M. Liam McGonagle's old solicitor's firm, Kennedy McGonagle Ballagh, acted in relation to the matter. Field-Corbett did not seek a fee.

According to the Ansbacher inspectors' report, Traynor set up his Cayman Islands trust, the Poinciana Trust, in May 1993, with the beneficiaries being Traynor and his wife, in the first instance, and the wider family in the second. The assets held by the trust included four Cayman companies, including Hamilton Ross Company Ltd and Poinciana Fund Ltd. According to the inspectors, Furze, acting as trustee of the Poinciana Trust, disposed of Hamilton Ross Company Ltd without telling the Traynor family, and without any money being passed on to the Traynor family. The Traynor family, according to the inspectors' report, said that they did not know when Hamilton Ross Company Ltd was sold by Furze, or the price paid, if any.

'The Traynor family have assured the inspectors that they do not have this information', the inspectors wrote. 'If the lack of knowledge of the Traynor family is genuine (a fact not disputed by the inspectors), the secret nature of this transaction is a lesson to those who entrust their wealth to offshore trusts.'

Barry Benjamin, the US national who is now looking after Hamilton Ross and other aspects of the Furze estate, has told the *Irish Times* that he believes Hamilton Ross never belonged to Traynor, and always belonged to Furze. In relation to the inspectors' comments about the Poinciana Trust, Benjamin said: 'I find the suggestion that Mr Furze might have made off with any of their (the Traynor family's) money laughable.' He said that the inspectors could imply whatever they wished. 'I have no desire to argue with them about it.' The Traynor family declined to comment on the matter.

In the wake of the publication of the inspectors' report it was said that the Ansbacher scheme was, of course, not the only tax-dodging scheme in existence at the time. There must, undoubtedly, be quite a number of such schemes which have not been discovered, and probably never will be discovered. Furthermore, the revelations concerning the extent to which people hid money from the Revenue in bogus non-resident accounts maintained in the main commercial banks, including the State-owned ACC bank, has illustrated the scale of the massive tax evasion which took place during the Ansbacher period. That said, however, the Ansbacher scheme was unique in that it included Haughey, Traynor, and people who gave money to Haughey by way of Traynor. There was a political stink about Ansbacher which, given Haughey's importance during the period, is unlikely to apply to any other tax evasion scheme which may yet be discovered.

These days the relationship between politics and money has changed. Much of what the more wealthy and privileged once did so surreptitiously is now done in full public view. The rich still don't pay the same percentage of their earnings in tax as the less well-off, but now it is because of non-residency status, legitimate tax allowances, and low capital gains tax rates. Government policies provide rich people with the opportunity to reduce their tax bills. The argument made by Haughey in the 1950s and 1960s, that people should be allowed keep more of their profits, has won the day. The management of the economy has become, perhaps, the key role of politics and politicians, and the politicians work closely with big business in doing so. Money remains crucial to electoral success, and money can still buy access to political power.

It's no longer a conspiracy, it's just the way things are.

Index

$$118$$

$$14 \overline{)1680}$$
$$14$$
$$\overline{28}$$
$$14$$

$$14 \overline{)1880}$$
$$14$$
$$\overline{48}$$

$$112 \overline{)1680}$$
$$112$$
$$\overline{80}$$
$$50$$
$$\overline{30}$$

$$124 \overline{)1680}$$
$$124$$

$$115$$

$$13 \overline{)1500}$$
$$13$$
$$\overline{20}$$

$$14 \overline{)1680}$$
$$14$$
$$\overline{022}$$
$$14$$